REASON AND WORLDVIEWS

Warfield, Kuyper, Van Til and Plantinga
on the Clarity of General Revelation
and Function of Apologetics

Owen Anderson

University Press of America,® Inc.
Lanham · Boulder · New York · Toronto · Plymouth, UK

Copyright © 2008 by
University Press of America®, Inc.
4501 Forbes Boulevard
Suite 200
Lanham, Maryland 20706
UPA Acquisitions Department (301) 459-3366

Estover Road
Plymouth PL6 7PY
United Kingdom

Library of Congress Control Number: 2008921686
ISBN-13: 978-0-7618-4038-1 (paperback : alk. paper)
ISBN-10: 0-7618-4038-9 (paperback : alk. paper)

⊖™ The paper used in this publication meets the minimum
requirements of American National Standard for Information
Sciences—Permanence of Paper for Printed Library Materials,
ANSI Z39.48—1984

CONTENTS

FOREWORD

Dr. Owen Anderson has ably analyzed the epistemology of B.B. Warfield in contrast to that of Abraham Kuyper and Cornelius VanTil. He has done this in order to draw attention to the necessity of clarity and inexcusability if the claims of historic Christian theism are to be meaningfully understood. Any thoughtful Christian apologetic must therefore begin with showing the clarity of general revelation in order to establish the inexcusability of unbelief. In philosophy, this intellectual endeavor has been the domain of natural theology. Dr. Anderson's analysis of Warfield has therefore shown the necessity for the project of natural theology.

Natural theology, I believe, is not only possible. It is necessary. The external and internal challenges to Christian theism have accumulated through the Enlightenment period, although they have roots going back into ancient history. The need for natural theology today is more urgent, if not acute, as ancient worldviews come face to face. All human beings need meaning, and neither skepticism nor fideism can provide that meaning for human beings as they become more epistemologically self-conscious and consistent. A deeper understanding of reason, leading to a deeper, clearer and more consistent understanding of good and evil, can lead us out of our present impasse, to a unity and fullness we had not thought was possible. In the present post-Christian, Post-Modern milieu, the necessity for natural theology has become pressing. Dr. Anderson's analysis of recent contributors to this dialogue is therefore both valuable and timely.

Surrendra Gangadean
Phoenix, AZ
October, 2007

PREFACE

The following revision is the result of having used *Benjamin B. Warfield and Right Reason* in a number of classes. In order to respond to questions and comments, I have made changes to the original text, but also added material about Reformed Epistemology, and the challenges from David Hume and Immanuel Kant.

The change in the title reflects a change of focus for the book. While the book continues to be an analysis of Warfield's view of apologetics, it has grown beyond this to be a critical appraisal of the current state of natural theology, and an examination of what is needed to address challenges to natural theology raised in the Enlightenment.

This book raises many questions that it does not answer. Specifically, having identified the challenges from Hume and Kant, and noted that their challenges have not been successfully addressed, I only hint at how to do so. I expect to remedy this in forthcoming works, titled *The Clarity of God's Existence: The Ethics of Belief After the Enlightenment* and *Religion and Reason in America*. I can point the reader to a book by Surrendra Gangadean, appearing in the Spring of 2008. It is titled: *Philosophical Foundation: A Critical Analysis of Basic Beliefs*. This book sets the context for the need for clarity, and works step by step through the process of critically examining the basic beliefs that serve as the foundations to worldviews. It addresses the challenges from the Enlightenment, Modernity, and other sources in a way that has not been done to date.

My hope is that this will be a starting point for readers of this book to engage in investigation and thinking about these problems. Why has the clarity of general revelation been ignored by Christian philosophers and apologists? And what is the relationship between clarity, inexcusability, and the Christian message of redemption? I believe these are vitally important questions for religious belief and I hope this book helps the reader to understand and explore these questions.

ACKNOWLEDGMENTS

I would like to thank Surrendra Gangadean for the many ways that he has contributed to this project. I am indebted to my students who have thoughtfully read my book and asked questions that required further research and improvement in order to explain the development of reason and worldviews at Princeton. I give special thanks to my research assistants, Brian and Arturo, for their generosity and assistance. Brian's careful attention to detail has been invaluable. It has also been a special pleasure to work with my Grandfather on this project, and receive his suggestions. And most importantly, I wish to thank Sherry, who read and listened to the many versions of this work, and without whose help it would not have been finished.

Owen Anderson
Arizona State University
Phoenix, AZ
October, 2007

CHAPTER 1: INTRODUCTION

There is general recognition of the plurality of worldviews to be found among human civilizations. But how are persons in different worldviews to come to agreement, and can reason be used to help in living the examined life and knowing which worldview to accept? What are the implications if one of these worldviews claims that all humans have failed to understand what is clear about God and man, good and evil, in the face of a clear general revelation and therefore need redemption?

Why should a person accept one worldview over another? What is required in leading the examined life? Christianity teaches that humans need redemption. This is redemption from not seeking, not understanding, and not doing what is right (Romans 3:11). This failure to understand includes the failure to understand God, and this is said to be inexcusable (Romans 1:20). The Apostle Peter encourages his audience to "always be ready to give a defense to everyone who asks you a reason for the hope that is in you" (1 Peter 3:15, NKJV). Such a defense is the goal of apologetics. Throughout the history of Christianity apologetics has been assigned different functions and importance. While these differences depend on various factors, central among these factors is how the apologist understands the goal of the Christian life and the need for the knowledge of God. In order to defend the faith the apologist must know what a defense is (what is "reason"), and the content of the faith being defended. In keeping with this admonition, Benjamin B. Warfield (1851–1921) gave a system of apologetics that centered its epistemology on the concept of "right reason." As the last of the Old School Princeton Theologians, Warfield argued that God's existence can be known by reason through general revelation (what can be known of God everywhere and at all times). This work will examine Warfield and his legacy specifically with respect to his claim that reason can be used to know God, and how this consequently gives to apologetics the task of showing the inexcusability of unbelief.

Reason and Worldviews aims to contribute to the study of Warfield and apologetics by examining the role of the knowledge of God and the inexcusability of unbelief in Warfield's system. Christianity claims that humanity is inexcusable in its ignorance of God's nature and power (Romans Chapter 1). The Apostle Paul begins his systematic statement of Christian doctrine (the book of Romans) by saying, "For since the creation of the world His invisible attributes are clearly seen, being understood by the things that are made, even His eternal power and Godhead, so that they are without excuse" (Rom 1:20, NKJV). What can be known of God is revealed to all in a clear general revelation. "The heavens declare the glory of God; And the firmament shows His handiwork" (Psalm 19:1, NKJV). This means that all people at all times can know God. Accordingly, it is the rejection of the knowledge of God as revealed in creation that leaves humanity inexcusable, and in need of redemption. Warfield echoes this when he says:

> This primary idea of God, in which is summed up what is known as theism, is the product of that general revelation which God makes of Himself to all men, on the plan of nature. The truths involved in it are continually reiterated, enriched, and deepened in the scriptures; but they are not so much revealed by them as presupposed at the foundation of the special revelation with which the scriptures busy themselves.[1]

One of the distinctive claims of Christianity is that all humans need redemption and that this redemption comes only through Christ. This claim carries with it some important assumptions. First, the need for redemption assumes guilt. That a person needs to be redeemed first assumes that the person is guilty of something. The Apostle Paul claims that humans are guilty in their failure to know God, and summarizes sin as not seeking, not understanding and not doing what is right. Second, if a person is guilty in his failure to know God this assumes that the person could have known God (as opposed to saying that he already knows God and the only problem is in his actions). Paul asserts that the truth about God is suppressed. Truth is suppressed by offering alternatives to belief in God. The implication is that there must be a general revelation of God to all humans in order for unbelief (alternatives to belief in God) to be inexcusable. This is stated in the definition of sin: not seeking, not understanding, not doing what is right. And third, this general revelation of God must be readily knowable, or clear, in order for there to be inexcusability, guilt, and the need for redemption. God's existence must be knowable through the use of reason by all humans. If it is not, then unbelief has an excuse, and the claim that humans need redemption from guilt is unfounded. This gives a very clear project for apologetics: to show that God's existence is knowable by reason through a clear general revelation to all humans so that unbelief is without an excuse. Without this foundation the rest of the Christian message about redemption and Christ will not make sense. It will be on this basis that Warfield, Kuyper, and Van Til are analyzed: to what extent does their epistemology and apologetical method support the clarity of general revelation as a necessary presupposition to the Christian message of redemption, and what role do they give to the knowledge of God in human life?

Princeton, Warfield and Reason

Warfield's emphasis on "right reason" is closely connected to the need for clarity and inexcusability, and leads therefore to his stress on the need for apologetics. At the same time, there are aspects of his approach that might lead to what is called "evidentialism." Evidentialism uses evidences to inductively arrive at the truth of Christianity, and consequently only establishes the *probability* of Christianity. The problem with this approach is that it does not establish the inexcusability of unbelief and therefore does not give the foundation needed for redemption. It is helpful to understand Warfield in the context of Princeton Theological Seminary, and Scottish Common Sense Philosophy, which was the epistemology of choice at Princeton. Princeton Theological Seminary's stated purpose was to educate youth for the ministry with an emphasis on understanding and defending the Reformed faith. In his essay on Warfield, W. Andrew Hoffecker notes that A. Alexander passed his mantle to Charles Hodge, giving with it the guarding of this original purpose.[2] The passing of A. Alexander's mantle to Charles Hodge, and then A.A. Hodge, is symbolic of the continuity of thought and agenda between these theologians. Princeton was proud that it had not changed in the face of continued intellectual attacks from sources such as Arminianism, Deism, and Unitarianism over the course of the 19th century. This tradition continued more or less consistently until 1929 when the faculty split and some left to start Westminster Theological Seminary to preserve what they believed to be the Princeton tradition.

Higher education began shorter after the founding of the first colonies. Harvard was founded in 1636. In 1642 eight laws to govern Harvard students were given. The second was: "Every one shall consider the main end of his life and studies, to know God and Jesus Christ which is Eternal life (John 17:3)." Yale and Princeton were started when their founders perceived that Harvard was no longer staying true to its original goals. Princeton College, a product of the First Great Awakening, had specific views of what it means to know God and these in turn had influence on Princeton Seminary. Early in the history of Princeton Seminary, Harvard Divinity School had hired Ralph Waldo Emerson and in doing so embraced his views of theology. Princeton saw itself as the continuation of the original charter of higher education in the colonies and the U.S.

The beginnings of new schools cannot only be explained in terms of a need for more ministers due to a growing and expanding population. If that were the case then the new schools could simply be expansion campuses of the original school. Instead, they each viewed themselves successively as correcting mistakes that had entered into their competitors. But why did such mistakes enter in, and were the solutions offered sufficient? Princeton Seminary itself had turned away from these original goals by the 1920's. This suggests that its solution to the problems at Harvard was not sufficient to keep Princeton itself from changing. The following will study how the approach of Princeton to the knowledge of God can help explain why it was unable to continue in that vision. The implication is that if such a vision is to be successful it must be built on a better foundation. Specifically, if Harvard and Princeton made the knowledge of God their goal, but were unable to sufficiently respond to challenges to belief in God, it is no wonder that such pressure made them abandon this goal. Can God be known?

The epistemology adopted by Princeton Theological lent itself to a defense of the faith in line with an appeal to reason and common sense. Thomas Reid developed the Scottish Common Sense Philosophy in the latter part of the eighteenth century. In it he argued, "Perception involves both sensation and certain intuitively known general truths or principles that together yield knowledge of external objects."[3] Reid argued this directly against the skepticism of David Hume, and Reid's system stands in contrast to Immanuel Kant's attempt at avoiding this same skepticism.[4] "I observed that Mr. Hume's argument not only has no strength to support his conclusion, but that it leads to the contrary conclusion."[5] Reid argued that these intuitively known truths are knowable by all normal humans. The Princeton Theologians took this idea and applied it to apologetics in order to support the claim that there is a clear, general revelation. This Common Sense Philosophy provided Princeton a unique epistemology that had important similarities with Augustine and Calvin.[6] The views of general revelation that Princeton rejected were those that said either general revelation is not clear and does not reveal God, or that general revelation is faint, revealing a little but not much. In contrast, Princeton Theologians like Charles Hodge argued that the revelation of God's nature is clear enough to hold men without excuse.

Princeton's view of the relationship between general and special revelation is also important. The Princeton Theologians argued against those who said that general revelation reveals the world while special revelation (redemptive revelation) reveals God and redemption, or that God can only be known through special revelation. In contrast to such positions, Warfield argued that one must first see that God exists in order to have the message of special revelation authenticated. And yet at the same time Princeton failed to successfully respond to challenges within society and within Princeton itself, so that in the 1920's it altered its doctrinal position. Understanding this change requires understanding why appeals to common sense are insufficient.

Common Sense Philosophy does have some ambiguities, especially connected to what "intuitions" are known by all. Reliance on these "intuitions" often leads to fideism (belief without proof), and fideism undermines the need for redemption by denying that there is a need for clear, general revelation. Because the Princeton Theologians argued that the knowledge of God is common sense, this will have bearing on their understanding of how God is known. One common position says that God is known through an innate knowledge that all humans have and suppress. This leads to a situation where people simultaneously know and do not know God. Or perhaps the intuition is a feeling, like love or forgiveness. However, the Apostle Paul states that much more can be known of God through general revelation than a mere sense of love (specifically, God's eternal power and divine nature). The relationship between the Princeton Theologians and Scottish Common Sense Philosophy helps to clarify their position while at the same time creating ambiguities central to the debate between B.B. Warfield and Abraham Kuyper.

Abraham Kuyper

While Warfield's emphasis is on right reason, Kuyper's emphasis is on the relation of beliefs to worldviews (*Weltanschauung*). It is on this point that the two thinkers differ. Kuyper emphasizes that a person's beliefs are a part of an entire worldview. Hence there is the worldview of believers, and the worldview of unbelievers. These two are irreconcilable, and they are directed toward different projects. What the believers call science, the unbelievers will deny as science, and vice versa. This view gives little importance to apologetics since while a believer may offer a sound argument to an unbeliever, the unbeliever will not recognize it as such. In general, arguments are unhelpful because the unbeliever will not recognize them as such given the non-theistic starting points. Indeed, Kuyper argues that the only way that the unbeliever can know anything is by being inconsistent with his/her own starting principles and relying on the theistic worldview. This inconsistency can be shown to the unbeliever, and herein is part of the job of apologetics.

Cornelius Van Til

The legacy of Warfield is not necessarily to be found at Princeton. In 1929 Princeton Theological split and a number of the faculty members left to form Westminster Theological. One of those that left Princeton to help found Westminster was Cornelius Van Til (1895–1987). Born in Holland, and having studied at Princeton, Van Til had a deep understanding of both Kuyper and Warfield. His Presuppositionalism is an attempt to find and emphasize the best in both, while avoiding what he saw as mistakes on each side. Specifically, while Van Til agreed with Kuyper that there are two worldviews existing in mutually exclusive spheres, and that only one is doing science, he agreed with Warfield that it is the Christian presuppositions that allow for knowledge. However, it is not the "right reason" that Warfield outlines, but the Bible itself that provides the foundation for knowledge. Van Til argued that God's revelation speaks for itself and provides the only possible basis for knowledge. The problem with this approach is illustrated in the following question: If Scripture is the only standard for knowledge, how are persons inexcusable for their unbelief? Warfield's appeal to right reason will provide the answer to this in that reason is not an arbitrary basis upon which to know God, nor is it only available to those with access to the Bible.

Reformed Epistemology

While not within the Princeton tradition, Reformed Epistemology claims to be the heir of the reformed discussion about belief in God. Alvin Plantinga claims that Christian belief in God is properly basic and warranted. This has some affinities with the claim that belief in God is common sense. Unbelief and the failure to know God are traced to improper function inherited from the Fall. But are the adherents of non-Christian worldviews also warranted in their beliefs? And how can unbelief be inexcusable if it is due to improper function outside the control of the person?

Natural Theology

While natural theology, or the study of general revelation, has generally been downplayed in the 20th century, how can the Christian claim that unbelief is a sin be justified apart from the existence of a robust and clear general revelation? Skepticism and fideism are often used to avoid the need for natural theology, both from Christians and non-Christians. Furthermore, persistent misunderstandings and misrepresentations of reason and clarity make the work of natural theology difficult. Part of what must be done is to clarify the program of natural theology and explain why skepticism and fideism are insufficient.

Clarity, Reason and Proofs

An important part of studying Warfield and Kuyper is to understand their motivation in doing theology and apologetics. If the goal of the Christian life is to go to heaven, and this can be achieved by believing that Christ died for one's sins, then what need is there for knowing God, or using reason to understand proofs that demonstrate what is clear? This goal (a direct vision of God in heaven) takes away the motivation for seeking to understand by making the knowledge of what is clear about God secondary, perhaps not needed at all, or perhaps available immediately (vs. mediately through proofs) in heaven. Those Christians given to the intellectual life might enjoy proofs and apologetics, but such will not be necessary for the great majority of believers, and even for intellectuals they are more of a hobby. It is said that people do not reason their way into heaven, and they do not convert on the basis of proofs.

It might be true that people do not convert on the basis of proofs; indeed, Calvinistic theology maintains that people convert after the regenerating work of the Holy Spirit and in response to the preaching of the Gospel. But what are they converting from? If they are converting from not seeking and understanding what is clear about God, the implication is that they begin to seek and understand. And since they failed to seek and understand what is clear, after conversion they begin to seek and understand what is clear. Furthermore, heaven (as the state after death but before the resurrection) is not given as the goal of the

Christian life in scripture. Instead, Christ speaks about eternal life as knowing God (John 17:3). This means that conversion involves a return to seeking and understanding what is clear about God in order to have knowledge of God. In the following we will see that the failure to keep this in mind contributes to the failure to clearly define the role of apologetics and give an adequate response to the challenges of Modernity (especially from Hume and Kant).

In order to know what is clear one has to be seeking, and in order to seek one has to believe that the goal sought for will bring fulfillment. Thus, the motivation behind seeking involves an entire worldview about what is real, what is good, and what brings lasting happiness. The claim that one does not need to prove that God exists in order to go to heaven is often focused on a view of heaven that is the fulfillment of worldly desires. This attempt to sidestep the need for proofs is therefore rooted in a failure to find knowledge of God fulfilling and worth seeking. This will lead to finding fulfillment in other ways, and also to not seeing the need for careful thinking about God and challenges to belief. This failure to think carefully will result in ignoring challenges and in making mistakes in responses, which in turn leads to further challenges. It is the fear of such results that will be the basis for seeing the need for careful thinking and a clear focus on how it is that knowledge of God brings fulfillment.

Conclusion

In conclusion, the need for rationality, clarity, and inexcusability will be explored. If Warfield's method of apologetics can help solve problems facing contemporary Christian apologetics, these assumptions of the Christian worldview must be better understood. The history and figures looked at in this account demonstrate how the notion of inexcusability in Christian apologetics has been developed in the Christian tradition up to the present. Concerning the role of apologetics, Warfield argued: "The part that Apologetics has to play in the Christianizing of the world is rather a primary part, and it is a conquering part."[7] Such a role cannot possibly be fulfilled if the content of the message cannot be known by reason. In contrast to the anti-rationalism of Kierkegaard and Neo-Orthodoxy, the Princeton Theologians, and later the Presuppositionalists, argued for the ultimate rationality of Christianity and the inherent inconsistency of all other worldviews. Christianity claims to have a message of redemption for all people. This assumes that all people need redemption. Warfield's method of apologetics is demonstrably more consistent with the assumptions behind the Christian message of redemption than are other methods. The following will explore his method, and draw out some implications about reason and general revelation.

Questions:
1. Why must God be knowable if the failure to know God is a sin?
2. What is the distinction between general revelation and special revelation?
3. If special revelation is about redemption, what does it presuppose?

4. What is assumed in the claim that humans need redemption?
5. What is the difference between mediate and immediate knowledge? How is God known?
6. What is conversion a return to?
7. What is the motivation for seeking? How is this an expression of a worldview?
8. What is the result of not seeking to find fulfillment in knowing God?
9. What was the original goal of Harvard, and why did schools like Harvard, Yale, and Princeton fail to maintain this goal?

CHAPTER 2:
PRINCETON THEOLOGICAL SEMINARY AND
COMMON SENSE PHILOSOPHY

Within the context of an expanding and growing U.S., Princeton Theological Seminary began in order to meet the need for new ministers. But if Christian ministers are to teach the redemptive claims of Christianity, then what will be their basis for claiming that unbelief is a sin? What foundation must be established in order to make sense of the Christian message of redemption?

Old School Princeton Theological Seminary stood out in its time for its dedication to training ministers to give a rational justification of the Reformed Presbyterian faith. One distinguishing mark of Princeton was its reliance on Reformed Confessions, particularly the Westminster Confession of Faith.[1] The first article of this Confession begins by saying: "The light of nature, and the works of creation and providence do so far manifest the goodness, wisdom, and power of God as to leave men unexcusable." In this section of the Confession is affirmed all that was derived above from Romans 1:20. God's nature is clearly seen by the light of nature (reason), in creation, and in providence. It is the failure to see the revelation of God in these that leaves humanity inexcusable and in need of redemption. Knowledge of how this redemption is accomplished is found only in the scriptures. However, reason, creation, and providence still clearly reveal God to all and continue as the basis for holding humans accountable for knowing their Creator. Indeed, throughout the Confession the emphasis is on the revelation of the glory of God in all aspects of creation. In this chapter it will be argued that Princeton Theological attempted to formulate an apologetic (influenced by Scottish Common Sense Philosophy) that upheld clarity and the ability to know God, and therefore also maintained, at least by implication, inexcusability with respect to unbelief.

The Beginnings of Princeton

As an educational institution, Princeton's philosophy of education was an outgrowth of its view of the goal of Christianity. Princeton Seminary began in 1812, although Archibald Alexander, one of its first professors, proposed the idea of a new Presbyterian Seminary in 1808.[2] Alexander said at the General Assembly of 1808 that "In my opinion we shall not have a regular and sufficient supply of well-qualified ministers of the gospel, until every presbytery, or at least every synod, shall have under its direction a seminary established for the single purpose of educating youth for the ministry, in which the course of education from its commencement shall be directed to this object."[3] Plans began to be set in motion for what would become Princeton Theological Seminary. The purpose statement was initially drafted by Ashbel Green in 1810, and was altered imperceptibly by the General Assembly of the Presbyterian Church in 1811. "This seminal document contained the philosophy of theological education which Alexander and his successors adhered to closely, a philosophy impregnated with Scottish Realism."[4] The plan of the Seminary included an article titled *Of Study and Attainments*, giving the objectives to be expected of students by the end of their third year. By this time the student was to "have laid the foundation for becoming a sound biblical critic; . . . a defender of the Christian faith; . . . an able and sound divine and casuist, . . . a useful preacher and a faithful pastor."[5] Marion Taylor, in the book *The Old Testament in the Old Princeton School (1812–1929)*, states that the intention of the biblical studies was not heuristic, but instead was a continuation of the philosophical presuppositions of the school focused mainly on apologetic functions. "Central to the seminary's mission statement was the training for gospel ministry of men 'to propagate and defend . . . that system of religious belief and practice which is set forth in the Confession of Faith, Catechisms, and Plan of Government and Discipline of the Presbyterian Church; . . . [and] to provide for the Church, men who shall be able to defend her faith against infidels, and her doctrines against heretics'."[6] Thus the central focus and role of apologetics was a direct implication of the philosophical presuppositions, particularly Scottish Realism and its claim that knowledge is possible. "The defensive or apologetic orientation towards the study of the scriptures which grew out of the seminary's mandate became one of the hallmarks of the Old Princeton approach."[7]

While Princeton Theological Seminary sought to make a defense of the Christian faith a foundational part of its education of ministers, the role for this seems to be related to the turning away of other seminaries as opposed to the need for it in the goal of the Christian life. Where other seminaries were viewed as having turned aside to false doctrine (e.g., Harvard and Unitarianism), Princeton wanted to be able to stand firm, and saw the need for a rational defense. But what is the role of such a defense in the life of a believer? Is it mainly against alternatives? Or is it directly connected to eternal life? Charles Hodge was proud that doctrine at Princeton had not changed while he was there, and this is indeed a difficult endeavor compared to the other major seminaries of his day. But did

Princeton teach that the goal of the Christian life is heaven to receive the blessing, and how does this affect education?

Princeton educated ministers, who in turn educated their congregations. What is a minister to teach the people about seeking and understanding, and what is the relationship between these and going to heaven? Or, what is the result of not seeking and understanding? The story of Princeton Theological Seminary is wrapped around its view of heaven and the need for reason. While it held strongly to the need for reason as opposed to other seminaries that had denied historic Christian teaching, it did not go as far as it could because it came short of understanding how eternal life is knowing God due to its view of heaven.

Scottish Common Sense Realism

Scottish Realism was a distinguishing mark of the Seminary. "Together with the apologetic bent of the proposed curriculum, this feature was consistent with the 'external' approach to knowledge characteristic of Scottish Realism."[8] Mark Noll, in his "The Princeton Theology" that appears in *Reformed Theology in America*, sees this philosophical influence as one of four points that stands out as distinctive of the Seminary. The other three distinctive points are the reliance on Reformed Confessions, inerrancy of Scripture, and the work of the Holy Spirit. Scottish Realism affirms the ability of humanity to know, and gives standards for what does and does not count as knowledge.

In his inaugural address of 1812, A. Alexander affirmed the possibility of knowledge and outlined a method for attaining the truth. First, a truth seeker had to ascertain that the scriptures do in fact contain truths from God; secondly, he also had to understand what these truths are. To accomplish the first, the student must study the canon of the Old and New Testaments, including their consistency, authenticity, and inspiration. An evidentialist approach was taken to establish the authenticity and inspiration of the scriptures, by considering miracles, prophecy, and the social and personal benefits of the gospel. Finally, Alexander faulted the deists and others for not holding scripture as the sufficient and authoritative rule of faith.[9] Herein is a clear statement of the epistemology of Princeton. There is a particular emphasis on evidences and proof. Warfield echoed this when he said that before a person can trust the scriptures as authoritative it must first be proven that they are God's Word, and that there is a God who can be known.[10] Thus, there is some standard for knowing that is not derived from Scripture but is used to know more basic truths such as "what counts as Scripture?" It is this source of knowledge that will be examined further in order to see if Princeton's form of "rationality" produces the clarity needed for inexcusability.

It follows from the importance of Alexander's influence as a founding professor at Princeton that his instructors had an indirect influence also worthy of note. Of particular importance to Alexander was William Graham (1746–1799), who had been instructed by John Witherspoon (1723–1794) in Scottish philosophy. Witherspoon brought this teaching with him to America from Scotland where he had been influenced by such thinkers as Francis Hutcheson (1694–1746) and Thomas Reid (1710–1796). Mark Noll sees this philosophy as attempting to "rescue the English 'moderate' Enlightenment of Isaac Newton and John Locke from the skepticism of David Hume and the idealism of George Berkeley."[11] Alexander expressed this position as including an affirmation of the "common sense" of humankind and its ability to verify the physical senses and intuitive moral sense. The tradition at Princeton Theological Seminary that started with Alexander passed next to Charles Hodge who was also heavily influenced by this Scottish philosophy. "Hodge's debt to the Scottish Philosophy appears most clearly in the opening pages of his *Systematic Theology* where, in oft-quoted lines, he likened the construction of dogmatic systems to scientific exploration."[12] Charles Hodge's son, A.A. Hodge, similarly accepted this philosophy. Warfield was taught this system by James McCosh who came to Princeton from Scotland in 1868, the year that Warfield began his undergraduate studies.

Mark Noll points out that the Common Sense Philosophy stands in an important relation both to the "moderate" English Enlightenment, and to David Hume's skepticism. George Marsden makes a similar connection, although he breaks the Enlightenment into four parts. The first "is the early Moderate Enlightenment associated with Newton and Locke—the ideals of order, balance, and religious compromise. Second is the Skeptical Enlightenment, represented best by Voltaire and Hume. Third is the Revolutionary Enlightenment—the search for a new heaven on earth—that grew out of the thought of Rousseau. And fourth is the Didactic Enlightenment, stemming from Scottish Common Sense thought, which opposed skepticism and revolution but rescued the essentials of the earlier eighteenth-century commitments to science, rationality, order, and the Christian tradition."[13] Marsden sees only the first and the fourth as having lasting influence in the United States. Important for this book is the assumption behind the first phase of the Enlightenment that humanity can know, and the refutation of Humean skepticism in the fourth phase by Thomas Reid (1710–1796).

Thomas Reid

Thomas Reid was educated at Marischal College in Aberdeen. There, he studied with Thomas Blackwell and George Turnbull. Turnbull affected Reid greatly with his argument that knowledge of the facts of sense and introspection may not be overturned by reasoning.[14] Reid himself thought that one of his major contributions was a refutation of David Hume's theory of impressions and ideas. Marsden sees this as following from Reid's firm commitment to induction and empiricism.[15] "Reid himself was a great admirer of [Francis] Bacon, the early seventeenth-century philosopher of science. The influence of "'Lord Bacon' on Reid, Dugald Stewart observed approvingly, 'may be traced on almost every page'."[16] Reid claimed that Bacon had taught Newton to despise hypotheses as fictions, and Newton in turn argued that the correct method of philosophy is the induction of real facts from observation and experiment. This sort of induction rests largely on the assumption that there are some certainties that serve as a foundation to all knowledge. "Typically these foundational certitudes include our states of consciousness (such as, "I am awake"), self-evidently necessary truths (such as 1+2 = 3), and perhaps those things evident to the senses ("I am sure I see a tree over there")."[17]

Hume pointed out that these could not be supported by the empirical method advocated by John Locke. Hume argued that men have no way of knowing if the information from their senses corresponds to some object outside of their mind. He rejected metaphysics and theology as impossible and prone to result in violence. While Hume paid careful attention to how the human mind works and the role of evidence in knowledge, he also argued against the possibility of certainty based on sense experience, or the use of sense experience to prove that God exists. Thus, Hume used reason to cast doubt on empirical evidence and consequently produced skepticism. Reid said that Hume "Tells us that 'this universal and primary opinion of all men [direct awareness of external objects] is soon destroyed by the slightest philosophy, which teaches us that nothing can ever be present to the mind but an image or perception."[18]

Reid responded to Hume's skeptical method, and in so doing made plain his intention to establish a foundation for knowledge. Reid argued that all reasoning is based on a foundation, and that the first principles that make up this foundation yield some conclusions that are certain. For example, Reid said, "It is therefore acknowledged by this philosopher to be a natural instinct or prepossession, a universal and primary opinion of all men, a primary instinct of nature, that the objects which we immediately perceive by our senses are not images in our minds, but external objects, and that their existence is independent of us and our perception."[19] Here can be seen something of the concern for rationality and certainty. Reid claimed that these first principles, or basic beliefs, are held as such because they are found in everyone, and those devoid of such beliefs would everywhere be considered a lunatic. He also claimed that they are the foundation of all reasoning. Reid objected to Hume's questioning of principles that Reid believed were foundational.

The problem is that what Reid considered to be common sense principles might not in fact be commonly held among all worldviews, and questioning their truth might very well be one of the roles of philosophy. While Reid affirmed that knowledge is possible, in contrast to Hume's skepticism, his view leads to a kind of fideism where certain beliefs are held as basic and not needing proof. The problem is that these beliefs are not agreed upon by every worldview, and in fact seem to differ from worldview to worldview, and thus the assertion of such beliefs without proof and in the face of challenges from other worldviews becomes fideistic. This leads to problems for Christianity because it does not affirm a clear general revelation and therefore cannot establish the inexcusability of unbelief or the need for redemption.

The German philosopher Immanuel Kant rejected Reid's response to Hume. Kant argued that the appeal to common sense is the means by which "The most superficial ranter can safely enter the lists with the most thorough thinker and hold his own . . . Seen clearly, it is but an appeal to the opinion of the multitude, of whose applause the philosopher is ashamed, while the popular charlatan glories and boasts in it."[20] For his part Reid admitted to being part of the popular view in saying, "On the one side stand all the vulgar, who are unpracticed in philosophical researches, and guided by the uncorrupted primary instincts of nature. On the other side stand all the philosophers, ancient and modern; every man, without exception, who reflects. In this division, to my great humiliation, I find myself classed with the vulgar."[21] Reid differentiated himself from earlier foundationalists by giving an expanded list of basic beliefs held by common sense. His concern was to establish certainty with respect to our knowledge of the real world, and he finds this in commonsense beliefs that are only doubted by some "Philosophers or crackpots." Kant's critique of Reid is insightful for some of Reid's commonsense beliefs, but not all. If the law of non-contradiction (not both *a* and *non-a*, in the same respect and at the same time) makes the list, it seems that it does so not because it is the belief of the multitude, but because the opposite is literally not thinkable (this is how Aristotle spoke of this law). And this seems to be the criterion Reid gave for his commonsense principles (they make thought itself possible), but whether each of Reid's commonsense principles fulfills this criterion is a different question. A number of the beliefs Reid considered common sense might actually be beliefs that can be doubted, and have been doubted, and stand in need of proof. The law of non-contradiction cannot be doubted because it is necessary for any argument.

These three philosophers, Hume, Reid and Kant, were held up as exemplars by their followers and their systems have been the basis for important aspects of Modernity: Hume's empiricism and rejection of metaphysics, Reid's common-sense realism, and Kant's distinction between the noumenal and phenomenal and reliance on practical rationality. While Reid maintained that belief in God is common sense, both Hume and Kant rejected the arguments based on reason that had been used to prove that God exists. Is Reid and an appeal to common sense a sufficient response to Hume and Kant? Can the systems of these thinkers be understood in terms of their own views of what brings fulfillment? And if they are shown to have not seen what is clear, what can explain such a mistake by persons who are thought to be brilliant?

As for Princeton Theological, the influence of Reid's thinking is reflected in the general attitude toward knowledge and the ability for all humans to know the same basic truths. The point here is not to show a specific connection between Reid and Princeton; other works have already attempted this. Instead, the goal is to show that there is a similar affirmation. Both affirm that there are basic truths that all humans in all places can know, and that rationality itself assumes some specific principles, the negation of which would stop all argumentation. Marsden said:

What view of faith and reason emerges from this evidentialist apologetic? On the face of it, it appears that these evidentialists thought that reason must play a very large role in support of faith. 'Without reason,' says Archibald Alexander of Princeton, 'there can be no religion: for in every step which we take, in examining the evidences of revelation, in interpreting its meaning, or in assenting to its doctrines, the exercise of this faculty is indispensable.' 'Reason is necessarily presupposed in every revelation,' echoed his famous student, Charles Hodge.[22]

Charles Hodge and Reason

Those skeptics who claim that reason cannot attain knowledge, or that there are no such universal principles, are assuming in their argument that argumentation is possible and that there is some standard for giving a sound argument. Hence, Hodge and others presented their view as the only possible one because the opposite is self-refuting. In his *Systematic Theology* Charles Hodge clearly affirms the role of reason. Christianity rejects rationalism in all of its forms, but it does not reject reason in the service of matters of religion.[23] In the first place, Hodge argued that reason is necessary in order to understand any revelation.[24] Revelation is a communication of truth, and presupposes the capacity to receive it. "Truths, to be received as objects of faith, must be intellectually apprehended."[25] If a proposition is meaningless, however important it may be, it cannot be the object of faith. The objects of faith are beliefs such as the immortality of the soul, or that God is a spirit. In believing these, a person is affirming their truth, and in so doing, a person affirms that he understands what objects of faith mean. It follows that understanding is necessary and essential to faith. "The first and indispensable office of reason, therefore, in matters of faith, is the cognition, or intelligent apprehension of the truths proposed for our reception."[26]

Hodge concluded this section by saying, "About this there can be no dispute."[27] This is not a dogmatic assertion but a necessary truth. One cannot argue that argumentation is impossible. If a skeptic presents an argument that concludes reason is not able to apprehend meaning he would expect his audience to apprehend the meaning of his argument. In essence, such a person uses reason to deny reason. What is found in Hodge is the claim that reason, to give a minimal definition, is that by which a person comprehends the meaning of a proposition. This is different than apprehending the truth, and it is more basic than apprehending the truth (one must know what a statement means before being able to decide on its truth). Hodge here argues that reason is necessary for faith because in faith some proposition is believed, and in order to do this, reason must be used to understand what the proposition means. Hodge's *Systematic Theology* was used as the text at Princeton even in Warfield's time. Neither A.A. Hodge nor Warfield wrote his own systematic theology because there was no need. Thus Hodge's view of reason can be said to have been Princeton's view.

How did Princeton understand the clarity of God's existence and the means for coming to know God? In what way are God's existence and nature known?

Hodge's systematic theology will again be the most obvious source. In it, he distinguished between three possible origins of the idea of God. The first is that the idea is innate, second that it is a deduction of reason, and third that it is a product of tradition.[28] He argued for the first against the last two. For the purposes here it is important to see what he meant by "innate idea" as opposed to a deduction of reason. Hodge defined innate as "That which is due to our constitution, as sentient, rational, and moral beings. It is opposed to knowledge founded on experience; to that obtained by *ab extra* instruction; and to that acquired by a process of research and reasoning."[29] Hodge argued that it cannot be doubted that there is such a knowledge, and that the mind is so constituted that it sees some things immediately in their own light.[30] In such cases, provided that a person understands what is meant, the truth will be grasped. These Hodge called intuitions, or primary truths, laws of belief, innate knowledge, or ideas.[31] To call a belief innate is to indicate its source. It does not imply that the mind is born with ideas, in terms of "'Patterns, phantasms, or notions,' as Locke calls them."[32] What Hodge meant is that the mind is so constituted that it understands some things to be true without proof and without instruction.[33]

The law of non-contradiction is necessary for argumentation itself. The law of non-contradiction is the case because the opposite is impossible. Reason, specifically the law of non-contradiction, plays an essential part in thinking. Hodge called reason the *judicium contradictionis*.[34] Because faith, which is the believing of a doctrine to be true, involves the mind, it is not possible to have faith in a doctrine that is contrary to reason. In this way, reason can judge what is and is not a special revelation. "We are, consequently, not only authorized, but required to pronounce anathema an apostle or angel from heaven, who should call upon us to receive as a revelation from God anything absurd, or wicked, or inconsistent with the intellectual or moral nature with which He has endowed us."[35] The mind of man is to be submitted to God, and this submission is absolute. What humans are submitting to is God's infinite wisdom and goodness. Hodge affirmed that it is impossible for God to contradict himself, and equally impossible for him to declare as true, through special revelation of any kind, what he has made it impossible for humans to believe by the laws of our nature.[36]

It is not the case that reason and the impossible are whatever seem difficult to believe for the culture or a particular person. While the law of non-contradiction is not arbitrary, often standards are set up that are arbitrary. "Men are prone to pronounce everything impossible which contradicts their settled convictions, their preconceptions or prejudices, or which is repugnant to their feelings."[37] Hodge gave as examples that the earth revolves on its axis and moves through space at a high speed. It is similar folly for men to reject the claims of scriptures because they do not fit in with their previous assumptions about what is practically possible. "The impossible cannot be true; but reason in pronouncing a thing impossible must act rationally and not capriciously. Its judgments must be guided by principles which commend themselves to the common consciousness of men."[38] In the contemporary age it may seem "impossible" to many that God created the world in six days. Yet this is by no means impossible in terms of being a logical impossibility, and to declare it as such is to use a cultural standard instead of reason. In an important way, Hodge's use of reason reflects how he and other Princeton Theologians responded to the liberal scholarship of the 19th century. Concerning such trends as higher criticism, evolution, and comparative religion, the Princeton Theologians consistently pointed out that these are expressions of the materialist, or naturalist,[39] worldview (see Hodge's *What is Darwinism?*). These trends are not "scientific advancements" in the way that Newton's explanation of motion was. They are the cosmological expression of a worldview. Thus, for a naturalist to claim that the creation account in Genesis is "irrational" is an example of begging the question, and the very kind of thing Hodge claimed is not a correct use of reason.

The role that Hodge gave to reason extends even to the judgment of special revelation. Hodge stated that reason is meant to judge special revelation. Such a revelation will not contain contradictions, and any revelation that does contain contradictions is not from God. It is reason's prerogative to judge the credibility of any revelation.[40] Reason judges what is impossible (that is impossible which contradicts itself), and this includes special revelation.[41] Hodge did not see this as setting a human standard to judge God. It was during this time (1800's) that "higher criticism" of the Bible became the popular trend in academic circles.[42] Yet the scholars who took part, and continue to take part, in that activity were not doing what Hodge outlined. The contradictions that Hodge was speaking of are not the contradictions such critics of the Bible look for. Hodge was speaking of metaphysical contradictions about being, while these critics look for what is "practically" difficult for their culture (worldview) to accept. When Hodge referred to reason, he was not speaking about "what people commonly believe." He was particularly talking about the law of non-contradiction. He saw this as part of the standard for knowing that God Himself gave to man. Therefore it follows:

> (1.) That is impossible which involves a contradiction; as, that a thing is and is not; that right is wrong, and wrong right. (2.) It is impossible that God should do, approve, or command what is morally wrong. (3.) It is impossible that He should require us to believe what contradicts any of the laws of belief which He has impressed upon our nature. (4.) It is impossible that one truth should contradict another. It is impossible, therefore, that God should reveal anything as true which contradicts any well authenticated truth, whether of intuition, experience, or previous revelation.
>
> Men may abuse this prerogative of reason, as they abuse their free agency. But the prerogative itself is not to be denied. We have a right to reject as untrue whatever it is impossible that God should require us to believe. He can no more require us to believe what is absurd than to do what is wrong.[43]

For Hodge (and the Princeton Theologians) there is, within Christian doctrine, no tension between reason and faith. People place faith in what they understand to be trustworthy, and understanding requires reason. Faith is not belief in what is absurd or self-contradictory. One does not have faith in square-circles, uncaused events, or that 2+2 is 5. One has faith in what is not seen, or even in what is practically impossible (vs. logically impossible) like the parting of the Red Sea. But in the context of Moses and the Red Sea the object of faith was that God would preserve His people, which is consistent given the nature of God and his promise to Abraham. The objects of faith can thus be judged by reason. Hence, faith in God requires that God's eternal power and divine nature can be known. Special revelation from God requires that there is a God. And so Hodge argued that God's eternal power and divine nature are known apart from special revelation. He asserted that all humans are bound by their very nature to believe in God, and that this cannot be avoided except through a derationalizing and demoralizing of their whole being.[44]

Hodge on Faith and Knowing God

Hodge believed that the existence of God is obviously manifested, by the entire creation, so that belief in God's existence is a natural product of the use of reason, as part of our very nature.[45] This is to say that God's existence is readily knowable, or clear to reason. It is not a deduction arrived at only after strenuous reasoning. It is not only for those minds that are able to leap nimbly through abstract thoughts. It is clear to all minds, however well or poorly educated. Hodge rejected the idea that belief in the existence of God is the result of a long chain of deductive reasoning.[46] It is not a generalization of science, like the law of gravitation, which is assumed in order to explain a large amount of phenomena. God is more than a first cause of the universe. Such theories are possible only for cultivated minds, and hence cannot account for the idea of God, and the belief in Him, found in the minds of all humans, even those with no formal education.[47] It does not require a university degree in order to apprehend God's existence. Hodge's claim was that God's existence is so clear that it is basic to other beliefs and knowable by all who think.

However, there is unresolved conflict in Hodge that resulted in a failure to explain the clarity of God's existence or its role in the Christian life. He says that reason is necessarily presupposed in every revelation, and that a proposition with no meaning cannot be an object of faith (which involves assent and understanding).[48] In faith we affirm the truth of a propositions believed, and we can affirm nothing of what we know nothing.[49] But then a problem arises in Hodge's thinking on this subject. He distinguishes between knowing on the one hand, and understanding and comprehending on the other. A person can know what the phrase "God is a spirit" means without comprehending God perfectly. He says we can rationally believe something to be, without understanding how or why. To some extent this is true, but if faith is seeking and understanding, can a person grow to learn the how and why? He goes further and introduces a new problem. He affirms that Christianity does not ask humans to believe what is incredible because what is incredible is impossible.[50] But then he says that a thing may be "strange, unaccountable, unintelligible, and yet perfectly credible."[51] Indeed, he says that unless we are willing to believe the incomprehensible we can believe nothing.

But what does this mean? Humans as finite cannot know any subject infinitely, including but not limited to God. Hodge does not seem to be answering an objection here, although he does say that it would be unreasonable to reject Christianity because it requires a belief in the incomprehensible. But what view says that humans can know everything? Hodge seems to fall into a kind of fideism here. He says that object of faith can be unintelligible, yet credible. If unintelligible, then how do we know what is being believed, what is the object of unintelligible faith? Furthermore, why accept unintelligible beliefs from Christianity and not from other religions?

If what Hodge is saying is that reason leads us to scripture, and then at that point we must accept unintelligible claims, he empties faith of content. If he is saying that God, as an infinite being, is incomprehensible and can never be fully known by humans, this is uncontroversial. The atheist does not reject belief in God because God is said to be incomprehensible; the atheist must also affirm that finite humans cannot know anything with infinite perfect. What this manifests is that Hodge allowed faith in the unintelligible, which undermines his own work about reason and God, and undermines the goals of Princeton. This mistake, combined with problems we will see in Warfield, produced a situation where Princeton Theological became unrecognizable in relation to its original doctrines. The position that faith can be in the unintelligible was rejected for theological liberalism because it gave at least the appearance of upholding intelligibility.

Hodge and Scripture

For Hodge the Bible was not the beginning of apologetics or the belief in God. The Bible itself assumes God's existence, and its message of redemption assumes sin. This sin is, at the basic level, a rejection of God and his revelation in creation and providence. Hodge believed that there is sufficient proof (clarity) that God exists: "The Bible regards unbelief as a sin, and the great sin for which men will be condemned at the bar of God. This presumes that unbelief cannot arise from the want of appropriate and adequate evidence, but is to be referred to as the wicked rejection of the truth notwithstanding the proof by which it is attended."[52] Hodge clarified that the claim that humans are not responsible for their faith arises from a confusion of ideas. Inexcusability does not apply to truths that are not clear, to speculative truths, or truths that require some matter of fact to know. "It is no sin not to believe that the earth moves round the sun, if one be ignorant of the fact or of the evidence of its truth."[53] But when unbelief is a sin, such unbelief has all the inexcusability that the sin brings with it.[54] Some beliefs can be maintained only by those having a reprobate mind, and that a person has such beliefs is evidence of their state.[55] The ignorance that humanity is inexcusable for having, is ignorance of the eternal power and divine nature of God.

Conclusion

Princeton held that humanity could know God. It is unbelief that is unreasonable, not belief. And it is this unbelief that is inexcusable. This implies that it is clear that God exists so that humans are without excuse in their unbelief. It is in this sense that there is a Christian apologetic. It is in this sense that special revelation makes sense (as redemptive revelation). The above establishes the foundation for the rest of this study. It not only gives some sense of Princeton's view of general revelation, but it gives the direction that apologetics is to take. Those who ask others to place their belief in the irrational are not doing apologetics (in the sense held to by Princeton). One who depends on irrationalism cannot argue that others should place their belief in one kind of irrationalism rather than another kind without becoming self-referentially absurd. Similarly, those who claim that knowledge is not possible are not in a place to give an apologetic. Apologetics assumes that reason can be used to know God, that God's eternal power and divine nature are clear, that the failure to see what is clear makes a person inexcusable and in need of redemption.

And yet, even with all of this going in its favor, Princeton was not able to maintain its position and in the 1920's became theologically liberal. Why? Above we saw that Hodge's view of faith allowed for belief in what is unintelligible. This stood in stark distinction with how he relied on reason in other areas. This coming short in understanding reason and intelligibility is a significant problem. It is with these issues in mind that Warfield's view of apologetics will be investigated.

Questions:
1. What were some of the founding ideals for Princeton Theological Seminary?
2. Why did Princeton believe that a rational defense is necessary, how could they have gone further with this, and what kept them from going further?
3. What is Common Sense Philosophy, and what does it say is common sense?
4. Why is Common Sense Philosophy insufficient to support the claim that unbelief is inexcusable?
5. Why did Hume reject metaphysics and theology?
6. What was Immanuel Kant's criticism of Thomas Reid?
7. Is Reid's common sense a sufficient response to Hume and Kant?
8. What was Charles Hodge's view of reason and general revelation?
9. According to Hodge, why is special revelation necessary?
10. According to Hodge, what is the relationship between faith and reason, and scripture and reason?
11. Why is Hodge's view of faith and reason problematic, and how might this have contributed to Princeton Theological changing its doctrine?

CHAPTER 3:
BENJAMIN WARFIELD AND REASON

Theologically, Princeton held to orthodox Calvinism. While some Calvinists were led to deny the importance of reason due to their understanding of the doctrine of the effectual calling, Princeton theologians affirmed the role of reason in knowing God and establishing the foundation for the Christian claims about redemption. Does the doctrine of total depravity assume a clear general revelation, and how has this been understood by the historic tradition as summarized in the Westminster Confession of Faith?

In the writings of B.B. Warfield there is a continuation of Hodge's thinking on apologetics. Warfield never wrote a systematic theology of his own, as Charles Hodge had already filled the need. Warfield was very prolific, however, contributing articles and reviews on numerous topics. He upheld the Princeton ideas of Common Sense Realism in his view of apologetics and how God is known. His debate with Abraham Kuyper forced Warfield to better articulate his, and Princeton's, view. Warfield's view of apologetics includes his definition of apologetics (somewhat different from Kuyper's), his understanding of rationality and the ability to know God, his view of clarity and inexcusability, and finally his understanding of the role of special revelation. Here it will be argued that Warfield affirmed that there is a clear general revelation of God to all humans, that humans can know God through the use of reason, and that by implication unbelief is inexcusable. Much of this is stated explicitly by Warfield, although some of it will be drawn out by implication. There are some problems that might arise due to an evidentialist influence in Warfield, and these will be considered in the conclusion.

Warfield and Apologetics

Warfield defined apologetics in his *Studies in Theology*. Here he differentiated between apologetics and apologies. Apologies are defined as defenses of Christianity in some sense or another. Apologetics, however, is the establishment of the knowledge of God that Christianity professes to embody and endeavors to make efficient in the world.[1] Warfield did not see the essential function of apologetics to be a defense, in which case it would largely be defined by its opposition. Instead, he defined apologetics as a constructive science that at times may need to defend itself but is largely concerned with the building of a system rooted in needs found in the human spirit. In this way it is not dependent on the reality of sin, but includes a knowledge that would have been important and necessary even if there had been no sin at all. It is in this context that Warfield made the claim "If it is incumbent on the believer to be able to give a reason for the faith that is in him, it is impossible for him to be a believer without a reason for the faith that is in him."[2]

Here Warfield distinguishes between blind belief and belief with understanding. He states that belief without content is meaningless, and if belief has content then this includes giving an explanation or reason for belief. Implicit in this is the relationship between seeking and understanding. If we do not seek then we will not understand, and understanding indicates seeking. Therefore, if we claim to understand we should be able to show how we sought and came to understanding. However, Warfield does not develop this, and there are indications in his own thought that he did not take the need for reason as necessary. Instead, he may have been willing to rest with "good enough" reasons, which could be a result of focusing on heaven as the goal, rather than knowing God in all that by which He makes himself known.

The differences below between Warfield and Kuyper, and then Cornelius Van Til's attempt to find a third position, revolve around the question of the function of reason, and whether reason can be relative to a worldview (in contrast to being necessary for thought itself). Reid and the Common Sense Philosophers were searching for transcendentals (necessary prerequisites for thought). Reid may have mistakenly included many more things into the area of "common sense" than belonged there, but his aim was explicitly to find those fundamentals that are necessary for thought itself and hence cannot be doubted because they make thought possible.

That Warfield took a position very similar to Reid's (in contrast to Kuyper and Van Til) is an important aspect of Warfield's thinking on apologetics. Warfield was concerned with worldview apologetics. Warfield was concerned with the building of a system, but he does not give apologetics the role of proving every tenet of Christianity.[3] He saw this as a vulgar rationalism.[4] One important point for this book is that Warfield's epistemology cannot be said to be either rationalist or evidentialist.[5] Warfield claimed that evidence must be interpreted, and hence cannot stand on its own. He also did not attempt to prove Christianity by breaking it into atomic doctrines and then proving each of these. Instead, he saw the role of apologetics as establishing the whole of Christianity as the only true religion.[6] Warfield did not do this in an arbitrary fashion, stating that Christianity is true and hence so are its details. This would be to leave Christianity as the "great assumption", and simply beg the question with respect to its truth. Every worldview claims to be correct, and to be the only system that allows for knowledge. But this is much different than showing such to be the case. Instead he used a method similar to Reid's in that he appeals to "right reason" as the necessary precondition for knowing, and then shows how this reason necessarily reveals God. Warfield established clarity just on this point in that argumentation is not possible without reason, and reason reveals God to all. In this function, apologetics lays a foundation on which theology is built, and the entire structure of theology is determined.[7] The function of apologetics is especially the establishment of a foundation on which the work of theology can be built.[8]

Warfield, Reason and Worldviews

Warfield did not simply place two competing worldviews next to each other and argue that they cannot communicate, as did Kuyper. Warfield's appeal to reason followed that of Hodge outlined above. It is not so much that reason is neutral (which is what Van Til rejects) as it is that reason is necessary and is common ground for all humans. Unbelievers use the law of non-contradiction, but they use it in a limited way. The law of non-contradiction is necessary if argumentation is going to take place. A common method for arguing is to show that the opposite of a claim is impossible and hence the claim must be true. It is by the use of this law that God is shown to exist. The opposite claims are self-contradictory. Hence, reason is not neutral. The unbeliever, however, does not use reason in this manner, and in neglecting to do so fails to know God. It is in this sense that Warfield claimed that the task of apologetics is to bring out clearly the reason for belief and to make its validity plain.[9]

Warfield was not claiming a neutral position where believer and unbeliever can meet. Reason is not neutral, and so the unbeliever is caught in a difficult position. If reason makes argumentation possible, then the unbeliever must recognize his need for reason. If reason also clearly and necessarily reveals God to the unbeliever, then he must accept this or give up reason. But to give up reason is to do so because of the dilemma just mentioned, which is to say that to give up reason the unbeliever must use argumentation. But argumentation assumes reason, and so the unbeliever is left with a self-refuting position. There is no escape from reason.

Reason, while not neutral in one sense, is common ground because it is universal to all humans. And, because reason reveals God's existence, there is a general revelation of God to all humans. All humanity can use reason to know God. Warfield explicitly states this when he asserts that the idea of God is a product of general revelation which can be known by all humans, and that it is not revealed by Scripture but rather presupposed by Scripture, as the foundation of the special revelation of God's grace to sinners.[10] The belief in God is a necessary belief because one must stop thinking (stop using reason) to avoid it. Warfield calls it an intuitive truth because it is an unavoidable belief.[11] If a person tries to understand anything at all, the starting point must be a realization of his own dependence.[12] This realization is coupled with the implication of there being one on whom all else depends and who is therefore not dependent on anything.[13] This is a sort of immediate perception, and Warfield saw the theistic proofs as developing this idea further.[14] He seems to have relied on the arguments for a sufficient cause of the universe, an intelligent author of the order and design seen in nature, the necessity of an infinitely perfect being, and a moral absolute to establish a moral law for humans as dependent moral beings who are able to feel responsibility and be conscious of moral problems.[15] We will consider some possible problems arising from his reliance on intuition and the theistic proofs in the conclusion of this work. However, the important point for consideration here is that Warfield believed it was both possible and necessary to give proof for God's existence and nature.

Reason, Clarity and General Revelation

While Warfield does not speak explicitly about clarity, his position implies that reason reveals more than just the bare existence of God construed as an unmoved mover, or a "higher power." Rather, as the Apostle Paul says in Romans Chapter 1, God's eternal power and divine nature are knowable from the things that have been made (the creation). This implies that the use of reason necessarily leads a thinker to the idea of God if its implications are followed. In Charles Hodge's *Systematic Theology*, and A.A. Hodge's *Outlines of Theology*, there is a general kind of argument that attempts to categorize worldviews with respect to their claims about "being" and "dependence." Warfield appears to take a similar approach. This method of classification identifies three "kinds" of nontheistic worldviews: There is the view which claims that matter is independent (material monism); the view that claims the self is independent (spiritual monism); and then the view that tries a combination of both (dualism). Materialists wish to locate in matter the eternal cause of being, and limit all knowledge to material objects/causes. The second worldview wishes to find in the self the eternal cause of being, and hence explain all phenomena in terms of minds and ideas. The third worldview tries a combination of the two with an emphasis on one or the other depending on the thinker. In Greek dualism, Plato emphasized the ideas and universals and Aristotle the objects and particulars. Such a brief look at these worldviews admittedly must simplify them. However the basic point is not lost; each tries to find what is "eternal" (independent/without beginning) in something other than God. That nothing can be said to be eternal except God is to say that each of these positions involves a self-contradiction.

The Princeton Theologians claimed that reason shows that only God is eternal. It cannot be said of any other being that it is independent and eternal. Warfield affirmed that God is a personal Spirit, infinite, eternal, and unchangeable in his being and in the attributes such as intelligence and will that belong to him as a personal spirit.[16] These attributes are known by humanity through general revelation, and are richly propounded in special revelation.[17] The above concern with metaphysical views is something that the liberal Christianity of Warfield's day wished to avoid.[18] "Liberalism, one of the 19th century theological fruits of post-Kantian philosophy, wanted to rid Christian theology of its 'metaphysical' elements. To Warfield, this was apostasy."[19] For Warfield, and the Princeton Theologians, an analysis of metaphysics was necessary because a thinker's metaphysical view will influence his interpretation of data and consequently his entire scientific approach.

In the above section are drawn out some of the good and necessary consequences of Warfield's position. For Warfield what can be known of God through general revelation is much more than a mere "higher power." It is a revelation of God as a Spirit, infinite, eternal, and unchangeable in being, wisdom, power, holiness, justice, goodness, and truth (Westminster Shorter Catechism #4). This is a further development of proof for God's existence in that it does not stop with a "first cause" or the equally nebulous term "higher power." The argument used by the Princeton Theologians (seen in both Charles and A.A. Hodge) is to point out the contradictions in all non-theistic claims and thereby establish theism (using the laws of excluded middle and non-contradiction). Again, this is something available to all humans, and thus all humans can come to the knowledge of God.

In light of the above it seems fair to say that Warfield believed in a clear general revelation of God's existence. His approach affirms that right reason reveals God. Hence all thinkers at all times can know God, and are responsible for knowing God. This is consistent with what is asserted in Psalm 19 and in Romans 1. The Psalmist says that the sun reveals the glory of God (Psalm 19). Thus, to worship it rather than its maker is an idolatry that can only be committed by not seeing what is clear to reason (that the creature is not the Creator and therefore not to be worshipped). The clarity of God's existence and nature leads to inexcusability. If humans as rational beings can use reason to know God and yet fail to do so, there is no rational excuse for their unbelief. Warfield's apologetic argued that there is inexcusability for this unbelief. His approach to general revelation and knowing God is consistent with the claim that unbelief is inexcusable and requires redemption.

The Westminster Confession of Faith

The Westminster Confession of Faith begins by saying: "The light of nature, and the works of creation and providence do so far manifest the goodness, wisdom, and power of God, as to leave men unexcusable" (Chapter 1). Thus, Warfield, following this tradition, preserved rationality, clarity, and inexcusability as essential features of apologetics. It is the denial or confusion of rationality, clarity, and inexcusability that leads to some of the problems in Kuyper's position that alarmed Warfield. It is also only in this light that the need for special revelation is seen. The Confession continues on to say: "Yet are they [light of nature, creation, and providence] not sufficient to give that knowledge of God, and of his will, which is necessary unto salvation" (Chapter 1). Indeed, according to the Confession God decrees all things for the manifestation of his glory. Special revelation reveals how God will redeem humanity from sin. This assumes there is sin that requires redemption. The sin of not seeing what is clearly revealed about God in general revelation is inexcusable and places humanity in need of redemption. Warfield affirmed this order between general and special revelation when he said that general revelation reveals the idea of God to all humans, while special revelation presupposes the idea of God and serves the purpose of communicating the grace of God to sinners.[20] This does not mean that humans as sinners can come to God through general revelation apart from special revelation, or can achieve redemption apart from special revelation. Rather, it affirms that special revelation is needed as a revelation about redemption because what can be known of God through general revelation has been ignored.

A.A. Hodge wrote a commentary on the Confession which was first published in 1869 and would have been influential on Warfield. A.A. Hodge discusses the history of the Westminster Confession, compares it to other confessions of the Reformation, and traces its early use in North America, indeed by "all the Congregational bodies of Puritan stock in the world."[21] He explains WCF 1.1 in the following way: "That the light of nature and the works of creation and providence are sufficient to make known the fact that there is a God, and somewhat of his nature and character, so as to leave the disobedience of men without excuse."[22] There are two issues to note here: first, that the light of nature makes known God "somewhat" known, as opposed to being a full revelation of God's eternal power and divine nature, and second the focus on disobedience rather than first and foremost unbelief.

A.A. Hodge considers three criticism of this portion of the Confession: first, the extreme Rationalists who hold that human knowledge is limited to the material world; second, that human knowledge in the present condition is limited to special revelation; and third, that of the deists and theistic Rationalists who hold that general revelation is sufficient. His understanding of WCF 1.1, and replies to critiques, would have been influential on Warfield's understanding of the same, and on Warfield's understanding of the role of natural theology and general revelation. Insufficiencies in A.A. Hodge would have been passed on to Warfield, and I will note how these appear.

A.A. Hodge argues against the extreme Rationalists by asserting that there is a universal agreement by humans in all ages that there is a God and the best scientists (like Newton and Faraday) believed in God; the creation and providence are full of design; the human conscience implies our accountability to a divine law giver. As arguments in support of the clarity if God's existence, and in rejection of extreme Rationalism, these are insufficient. An appeal to universal opinion, the design argument, and human conscience cannot support the clarity of God's existence, and can be used by many non-theistic, non-Christian religions in support of their beliefs. Furthermore, Hodge, having lived after Hume, should be aware of how these arguments were challenges and rejected, and thus should know that his response is insufficient. This failure to be aware of the best challenges to theistic belief is part of the problem. It is revelatory of a lack of concern at some level; if life and death were in the balance of knowing and responding to challenges then more attention would have been paid to being aware of the challenges and responding in a way that show them to be clearly false.

A.A. Hodge responds to the second issue, that knowledge of God can only come from scripture, by noting that this is contrary to scripture itself (Romans 1:20–24), that there are many arguments for a First Cause who is at the same time a personal Spirit and moral governor, and that all nations (even those without special revelation) have had a knowledge of God. The appeal to Romans 1 is helpful, but needs to be further explained. Is the knowledge of God intuitive/direct, or inferred from the things that are made? Is it full and clear, or bare and minimal? Is it necessary for the blessed life, or secondary to a direct vision of God in heaven?

His second response is unhelpful. He asserts that the argument used to prove a first cause that is also a spirit and moral governor remain (in his day) unanswered. And yet Hume is believed to have devastated these arguments, and Kant rejected them as unable to give knowledge of God. Why didn't Hodge engage with these challenges? The answer must be in an attitude toward the role of general revelation. If the purpose of natural theology and the study of general revelation is to help humans as they prepare to go to heaven, then it is secondary and this attitude will permeate the quality of work that is done.

His third response, supposedly based on Romans 1, that all human societies have had a knowledge of God, is problematic. If all humans know God, then in what way do they suppress this knowledge? If they know God, then why are they inexcusable? Is it that they do not have special revelation of God? But in Romans 1 the discussion is about general revelation. The only answer can be that they do not know God, and suppress the truth of God with a lie. They believe this lie to be true, and replace belief God with belief in other worldviews. To assert that all humans have had a knowledge of God (vs. a revelation that would enable them to know God if they were seeking) is to undermine the claims made by Paul in Romans 1. He does note that all human societies have been truth mixed with error, but this comes in his discussion of why special revelation is necessary, rather than as an indication of how all societies have failed to see what is clearly revelation in general revelation.

A.A. Hodge responds to the third issue, that special revelation is not necessary because God is knowable from general revelation, is that this is rejected by scripture itself, from the fact of man's moral relationship to God, and the reality of incompleteness and error in all human societies. This last response would be very helpful as proof that no one seeks, understand, or does what is right. But used here it undermines the need for scripture. If human knowledge is incomplete and mixed with error because they need special revelation, and most humans have not had access to special revelation, then they cannot be held guilty or inexcusable. To appeal to scripture to justify the need for scripture begs the question. But his second response is helpful: Humans need special revelation because of their moral condition (inexcusable) before God. Because humans have failed to seek, understand, and do what is right, they need redemptive revelation, and since they have failed to seek and understand general revelation, this redemptive revelation must be given by God in the form of special revelation. Furthermore, how God will respond to mankind in sin is not something that could be deduced from general revelation even if humans were seeking. The reality of sin, the failure to seek and understand and do what is right, indicates a need for additional revelation about how God will respond to the rejection of general revelation. That content cannot be found in general revelation precisely because it is about the rejection of general revelation. But the Christian, restored to seeking and understanding, is all the more responsible to give a full and clear account of general revelation.

Warfield and the Relationship between General and Special Revelation

How did this affect Warfield's thinking about the clarity of general revelation? He notes in his work on the Confession that the natural knowledge of God is insufficient for attaining eternal blessedness.[23] Indeed, he says "the *religio naturalis* is, therefore, not *salutaris*, and avails only to render man, if he does not receive revelation, inexcusable."[24] Problematically, he maintains that the natural man cannot comprehend what he ought to comprehend of God.[25] This is extremely problematic because it means that while humans ought to comprehend God, they cannot. How can they be held responsible?

Warfield gives two reasons why general revelation is important: it awakens man to his need for special revelation, and it prepares man to understand special revelation. These could be helpful, as will be explained in a moment, but as Warfield expounds them they are undermining. It points man to special revelation by helping him rightly understand what it means for God to exist, and additional what is necessary for redemption. This could be helpful in maintaining that knowledge of God as Redeemer is only found in special revelation, but is necessary because God's eternal power and divine nature have been clearly revealed in general revelation but rejected. However, this does not appear to be Warfield's view. Instead, for Warfield special revelation is necessary for an understanding of God's existence. Indeed, he says:

> Thus only as faith in revelation does religion become what it should be, according to its conception: not a knowledge of God, nor yet an observance of the divine commandment in itself, but a determination of immediate self-consciousness, a feeling (Schleiermacher) which rests on the experience of God as absolute love.[26]

While potentially helpful, Warfield's claim that general revelation is necessary for special revelation undermines the Christian message of redemption. This is helpful if it is used to say that because humans have failed to seek and understand and do what is right, there is a necessity for special revelation to give a knowledge of redemption. It is true that this is a further revelation of God's nature, specifically his justice and mercy. But how does this relate to the original state of man? If the fullness of the blessing can only be had through special

revelation, how can persons be said to be inexcusable? And what is this fullness? We'll trace this further in Warfield's exposition of the first question of the
Shorter Catechism. But first it is important to note his reliance on Schleiermacher. Is the highest expression of religion the experience of God, which is an
experience of absolute love? Is this sufficient to distinguish Christianity from
other religions, and is it sufficient to support the claim that unbelief is inexcusable? Schleiermacher speaks of a sense of the other, and the experience of absolute love, but what content comes with this experience? This experience has
been interpreted in many different ways by many different worldviews/religions.
Is it in itself the highest expression of religion, or is the correct interpretation
and understanding of this the highest expression of religion? And by what standard do we interpret? These questions are not addressed by Warfield and are
indications of how he came short and why his method of apologetics was not
sufficient to protect Princeton from the challenges of Modernity. Indeed, the
fullest expression of Harvard's change came when it embraced Emerson in the
divinity school—but how different is Schleiermacher from Emerson? If Warfield is embracing Schleiermacher, the implication is that Princeton has changed
from its original view of how God is known and what the goal of the Christian
life is.

Warfield and the Blessing

A clear understanding of Warfield's view of the blessing is found in his exposition of the first question of the Westminster Shorter Catechism. Warfield
notes that no Catechism begins on a higher plane than does the Westminster
Shorter Catechism.[27] It begins by asking "what is the chief end of man?" and
answers "the chief end of man is to glorify God and enjoy Him forever. By contrast, the Heidelberg Catechism begins with human comfort, and can give the
impression that God's purpose is to comfort man.[28] He traces this to Calvin, and
from Calvin to Augustine.[29] Here we get a clear view of how Warfield understood "to glorify God and enjoy Him forever." Indeed, no Christian of any de-
nomination would deny that this is the highest calling of man. But once we
move past initial agreement to ask how this is done we get into the multitude of
divisions.

In appealing to Augustine, Warfield quotes some of the famous passages of
Augustine's that would receive universal agreement: "Thou hast made us for
Thyself, O Lord: and our heart is restless till it finds its rest in thee"; "Let God
be all in all to thee, for in Him is the entirety of all that thou lovest"; "if thou
dost hunger He is thy bread; if thou dost thirst He is thy drink; if thou art in
darkness, He is thy light."[30] But then the particulars of how Augustine understood this blessing becomes more clear:

> When he who is good and faithful in these miseries shall have passed from this
> life to the blessed life, then will truly come to pass what is now wholly impos-
> sible—that a man may live as he will. For he will not will to live evilly in the

midst of that felicity, nor will he will anything that shall be lacking, nor shall there be anything lacking which he shall have willed. Whatever shall be loved will be present; and nothing will be longed for which shall not be there. Everything which will be there will be good, and the Supreme God will be the supreme good, and will be present for those to enjoy who love Him; and what is the most blessed thing of all is that it will be certain that it will be so forever.[31]

The blessed life is in the next life. This life must be endured, and hope is placed in the afterlife which will last forever. The enjoyment of God, and his glory, are disconnected from this life and made otherworldly. There is no mention of the resurrection, and no mention of the cloud of witnesses that did not receive the promise at death but is said to be currently awaiting the finishing of the work (as opposed to being in a final blessed state in heaven—Hebrews 11). This is the influence of Plato on Augustine: the needs of the body and this world keep the mind from the perfect happiness of knowing the forms; release from the body allows the mind to have this direct apprehension of the forms. Here are two mistakes that are rejected by historic Christianity and the Westminster Confession: the body is evil and the cause of keeping men from God; direct (immediate) apprehension of God when released from the body is the source of blessedness.

In contrast to this, the Confession maintains that "it pleased God the Father, Son, and Holy Ghost, for the manifestation of the glory of His eternal power, wisdom, and goodness, in the beginning, to create, or make of nothing, the world, and all things therein whether visible or invisible, in the space of six days; and all very good (4.1). According to the Confession, the Fall was not due to the body, but "God was pleased, according to His wise and holy counsel, to permit [the Fall], having purposed to order it to His own glory" (6.1). Indeed, this sin occurred in a condition where all physical needs were met. The root was a failure to see through the temptation "you shall be like God," which cannot be blamed on bodily needs but on failing to seek and understand. Indeed, sin is defined first in these two terms (not seeking, not understanding), rather than in bodily terms. At the resurrection of the dead, "all the dead shall be raised up, with the selfsame bodies, and none other (although with different qualities), which shall be united again to their souls forever" (32.2). The change at death (for the believer), and in the resurrection, is a change to a perfection in holiness (32.1). But is this change affected apart from being restored to seeking and understanding? And is the beholding of God a direct vision (the beatific vision), or is God's glory seen in his works? If it is a direct (immediate) vision of God, this cannot be had until death, and what happens at the resurrection—is it lost when the soul is restored to the body? What value is in this world and the glory it reveals if the highest blessing is in the direct vision of God obtainable only out of the body? Indeed, the Confession seems to teach that highest end of man is to know the glory of God, which is revealed not directly but through the works of God. Knowing this requires a study of the works of God (creation, providence, redemption), and cannot be by-passed in favor of a direct vision.

Warfield, Augustine and Romans 1

Augustine's own conversion witnesses to why he came short in affirming the clarity of general revelation and the need to know the glory of God through the works of God. Having wrestled with Manicheanism, he rejected it as he became convinced that evil is not a being but the lack of being. Still not sure about leaving behind his former life, he hesitates until a time when he is sitting in his garden and hears a voice say "take and read." He picks up the Bible and reads Romans 13:13–14. This passage focused on the sins of orgies, drunkenness, sexual immorality and debauchery, dissension and jealousy. The Apostle Paul encourages Christians to turn from these things, but chapter 13 must be read in light of chapter 1. In Romans 1 Paul claims that although the eternal power and divine nature of God are clearly revealed so that unbelief is without an excuse, humans have suppressed the truth by their wickedness, and exchanged the glory of God for images of men and animals. So, while at one time they had known God, they exchanged this for belief in idols and used these false beliefs to suppress what is true about God. The consequence was that God gave them over to shameful desires and sexual immorality. It is in this context that Romans 13:13–14 should be understood; orgies, drunkenness, and sexual immorality are the result of having been given over by God because what is clear about God has been rejected in favor of idolatry (a false worldview). It is through the grace of God that humans are restored to being able to seek, understand, and do what is right.

But in Augustine's conversion, it is as if the sinful desires are equated with the body, and the sin of not seeking and not understanding and therefore misusing the body is not taken into account. Or, the relationship between not seeking, not understanding, and misusing the body is not affirmed to the extent that he rejects Platonic influence due to its inconsistency with Christianity. Rather than seek blessedness apart from bodily desires, Paul is arguing that failing to seek and understand result in being given over by God, and the grace of God not only restores humans from unrighteousness by also to seeking and understanding. Augustine, having been restored, should be able to show that Platonism is clearly false, that the Platonic view of God is not the same as God revealed in general and special revelation, and that his failure to know this was a sin. Augustine's longing for the direct vision of God in the next life has had serious implications for Christianity, and is found in Warfield's understanding of the Shorter Catechism.

The implications for Warfield and Princeton, coupled with the problems discussed earlier in Hodge's view of faith, help make sense of why Princeton underwent a change from its original vision, and why its vision was not sufficient to respond to challenges. It is one thing to say that only Christianity is rational, or that all other views are somehow irrational. It is another thing to show this. And it is still a further thing to show why this is necessary. Is this something every Christian must know, or is it enough for the majority of Christians to rest at ease in the comfort that their ministers know this? What is the connection between knowing what is clear about God and the blessed life? If God is known only through his revelation (not directly or immediately), and eternal life is knowing God, then anyone who wants eternal life must come to know God through his works and not place their hopes in an immediate vision of God in the afterlife apart from his works. By not developing this Warfield gives no motivation for seeking to use reason to understand God or the clarity of God's revelation. Without this motivation, it is no wonder why Christianity is largely unaware of Warfield and his work in apologetics, and that Princeton rejected its tradition in favor of one that it believed made better sense of this life.

Conclusion

In Warfield's view, general revelation reveals God's nature. However, this revelation has been denied so that it can be said "none seek, none understand, and none do what is right." God's plan for redemption thus presupposes that there is sin that requires redemption. It is in this sense that Warfield says that special revelation is necessary. Special revelation is necessary to make known the plan of redemption that reveals the depth of the divine nature.[32] That knowledge which the scriptures give cannot be found in general revelation.[33] But this does not mean that general revelation is somehow weakened or blurred after the Fall. Reason still reveals God as necessarily as before. And yet with all this in favor of Warfield's view, we saw that his reliance on Augustine, and Augustine's insufficient understanding of the blessed life, undermined Warfield's ability to make a connection between using reason to know God through his works, and enjoying God.

In light of this, the issue is whether or not humans will use reason to know God through his works. Is this necessary for the Christian life, or an extra hobby for some Christians? With these essential features of Warfield's position in mind, his debate with Abraham Kuyper (and later Cornelius Van Til's assessment of the two) will serve to show that the differences between these thinkers can be best understood in terms of their ability to defend the claim that God's existence is clear to reason so that all humans are inexcusable in their unbelief.

Questions:
1. What does Warfield mean by "right reason"?
2. Why does inexcusability require clarity?
3. How does the Westminster Confession of Faith understand the relationship between clarity and the need for redemption?
4. How did A.A. Hodge explain the first section of the Westminster Confession? What challenges to this did he analyze, and why were his responses insufficient? How did this affect Warfield?
5. In what way might Warfield's view of the goal of the Christian life have kept him from developing reason and the role of apologetics more fully?
6. What does the Shorter Catechism say is the chief end of man? How does Warfield understand this?

7. What was the central factor in Augustine's conversion? How did this limit his view of eternal life and the knowledge of God?

8. In what way did Augustine's view of the afterlife contain influences from Platonism?

9. How is God known, according to Augustine, in the afterlife? Why does this take away motivation to knowing God through his works of creation and providence?

10. According to Paul in Romans 1, what is the relationship between not seeking and understand, and then not doing what is right? How does this make sense of Romans 13:13–14 which was so influential for Augustine?

11. How did Warfield's reliance on Augustine create a problem for his view of the knowledge of God, and for Princeton Seminary?

CHAPTER 4:
ABRAHAM KUYPER AND WORLDVIEWS

The Dutch Calvinists looked to the Heidelberg Catechism as a summary of Christianity. While the Westminster Confession begins with the clarity of general revelation, the Heidelberg Catechism begins with the comfort of man and the need for regeneration. This difference in focus led to a different understanding of the role of apologetics and its relationship to the work of the Holy Spirit. Why do humans need regeneration? What sin have they committed? What does it mean to say that humans have failed to seek and understand?

The relationship between B.B. Warfield and Abraham Kuyper was one of mutual respect. Warfield was instrumental in getting Kuyper to give the Stone Lectures at Princeton in 1898, and then translating these into English. These lectures are now found in the volume titled *Lectures on Calvinism*. However, they disagreed on a number of significant points including apologetics. Although Kuyper did make important contributions to apologetics in terms of his analysis of worldviews, he did not maintain inexcusability precisely because he did not maintain a clear general revelation or rationality that is able to know this revelation.

Warfield, in an introduction to Francis Beattie's *Apologetics*, took the time to address what he thought were the failings of Kuyper's view on apologetics. Warfield was specifically concerned with the small role Kuyper gave to apologetics:

> It is a standing matter of surprise to us that the brilliant school of Christian thinkers, on whose attitude towards Apologetics we have been animadverting, should be tempted to make little of Apologetics. When we read, for instance, the beautiful exposition of the relation of sin and regeneration to science which Dr. Kuyper has given us in his *Encyclopedia*, we cannot understand why he does not magnify, instead of minimizing, the value of Apologetics.[1]

Warfield saw the cause of this small role for apologetics in Kuyper's system as the distinct contrast Kuyper makes between "the two kinds of science."[2] The product of the sinful man is different in kind than the product of the regenerate thinker. This is the essential difference between these two thinkers, and at its center is the reality that Kuyper's system did not preserve rationality and clarity.

Abraham Kuyper and Apologetics

The role Kuyper assigned to apologetics followed from his view of epistemology in general. Thus it makes sense to look at how Kuyper built a theory of world and life views that makes apologetics, and reasoning (in one sense) helpless. The notion of "worldviews" is central to Kuyper's thinking. "This concept is so fundamental to his thought, so important to his career and so central to his international legacy that 'Kuyper' and 'worldview' are virtually inseparable."[3] The question becomes whether there is any similarity between the believer and unbeliever with respect to knowledge. "The epistemological question which lay at the heart of the division between Kuyper and Warfield was whether or not the acquisition of knowledge was exactly the same in principle for the regenerate and the unregenerate mind."[4] Van Til explained that Kuyper denied any point of neutrality between the Christian and the non-Christian that could be used as a point of contact for debate.[5] Van Til's development of Kuyper will be the focus later and so without going into his view it is relevant to note here that Kuyper (and Van Til) claimed that the only way a non-theist can know anything is by borrowing from the theistic worldview.[6]

Kuyper agreed with the Protestant tradition in saying that all that is known of God is from God's revelation to us. There is no beatific vision where God is seen directly, apart from his work. "All knowledge of God must ever be the fruit of self-revelation on His side."[7] There is a difference between knowledge and belief. The unbelievers are in a state of believing propositions that are false. That is, they violate the standard or method for knowing. But, of course, they would not admit that they do this. The unbelievers, as well as the believers, both think that they are doing what it takes to gain knowledge. The former are incorrect about this, the latter are correct. In this sense there are two "kinds" of people. Kuyper divided them into those who admit of more than the natural world as a source of knowledge, and those who admit of only the natural realm:

> This naturally all falls away when you encounter a difference *of principle*, and when you come to deal with two kinds of people, i.e., with those who part company because of a difference which does not find its origin within the circle of our human consciousness, but *outside* of it. And the Christian religion places before us just this supremely important fact. For it speaks of a regeneration, of a 'being begotten anew,' followed by an enlightening, which changes man in his very being; and that indeed by a change or a transformation which is effected by a supernatural cause.[8]

Worldviews and Starting Points

How can these two worldviews justify their starting points? Kuyper did not think this was an unfair question for one worldview to ask another.[9] He did, however, claim that one starting point cannot be used to judge another starting point.[10] The natural man, with his materialist assumptions, cannot judge the reliability of the theist and his assumptions (which for Kuyper are those found in special revelation).[11] This is essentially the way that the evolution/creation debate has been waged. The evolutionist will demand a material cause for all phenomena, and the creationist will insist that there are non-material causes that can account for the phenomena. Such a debate cannot be settled unless the issue of material/non-material causes is first decided.[12] These two cosmologies are parts of the worldviews Kuyper was speaking about. There is an "abyss in the universal human consciousness across which no bridge can be laid."[13] This abyss, for Kuyper, finds its origin in the regeneration that calls some from their sin to know God.[14] While Warfield agreed that it is necessary, in the fallen state, to be "reborn" in order to know God, this rebirth is a restoration of the use of reason in a person. Hence, the apologist can use reason to show that the unbeliever's worldview has no consistency and in this way "demolish the strongholds" of the unbeliever. Kuyper, on the other hand, saw such argumentation as useless.[15] But Warfield did not see the role of the apologist as the one who gives life; that is the work of the Holy Spirit. It is the role of the apologist to speak the truth, to use reason against the unbeliever's worldview, and it is through these means that the Holy Spirit works.[16] While the Apostle Paul cannot give a new mind to fallen men, he can preach the Gospel in the hope that the Holy Spirit will use this work. And at Mars Hill in Athens the Apostle Paul addressed the Greek philosophers of his day by arguing that if they wish to understand life, motion, and being they must first understand God's existence (Acts 17:28). This difference with respect to the role of apologetics finds its beginning in a difference over the nature of reason. Kuyper's division of humanity into two groups leaves reason helpless.

The Incommensurability of Starting Points

Kuyper believed that these two kinds of people operate with different principles. The basic principles of a system determine the manner in which the system will be developed. This is similar to Reid's foundationalism. Each system has foundational principles. However, unlike Reid, Kuyper did not think that these are "common sense." These principles are not agreed upon by all humans. Actually, the fallen men have one set of principles, but the regenerate have a different set of principles. This results in two different standards for knowledge. In an important way this is a direct contradiction to Reid's common sense philosophy. Because all beliefs are relative to a worldview, there are no "common sense" beliefs that transcend all worldviews. There is no neutral position on which these two worldviews can agree. Kuyper's emphasis is that there are two kinds of people that are distinguished by their starting points.[17] These different starting points result in a different content rising from consciousness, a different point of view about the cosmos, and consequently different actions. For Kuyper, this leads to two kinds of human life, and two kinds of science to support that life.[18] Thus any attempt to find a unity of science leads to a denial of the fact of palingenesis (rebirth), and consequently a denial of the Christian religion.[19]

The result of the two kinds of epistemologies is the division in "science" mentioned just above. Neither kind will admit that the other is really doing science because both operate with different principles that arrive at different conclusions. These principles are interpretive in that they are not derived from data but are used to understand the data. Hence there is no neutral data that can be referred to in order to prove one science is better than the other. Kuyper did not argue that there are two coherent explanations of the cosmos that can both explain what "is" with radically different representations.[20] He insisted that truth is one, and hence science is really only one.[21] Kuyper did not mean that different scientists have arrived at different conclusions that contradict each other and hence cannot both be true. What he meant is that both the believer and the unbeliever, operating with different starting points, wish to investigate the object and in doing so wish to offer a systematized account of what exists.[22] There may seem to be a similarity between the two kinds of people, and they may even live together in unity to some extent. However, the different starting points guarantee a difference in terms of method and inference. The conclusions arrived at will be influenced by the difference in method. In one sense this is a coherentist view of knowledge. The unbelievers arrive at knowledge by being consistent with their first principles. The same holds for the believers. But Kuyper did not want to admit that the unbelievers have knowledge in the sense of a true, justified belief. While their beliefs may be consistent with their first principles, they are not true because their first principles are not true. Hence, the problem is in the principles. Kuyper said that whatever the formal similarities in their work, they are running in opposite directions because they have different starting points. And because of this difference they approach their work with different motivation and different perspectives about its purpose and goal. The difference in starting points affects the entire system that follows from the starting points, and results in a difference in all aspects of life.[23]

Common Ground and Common Humanity

Kuyper did not argue that there is nothing in common between the two kinds of people. Everything is not a matter of worldview relativity. Some things, like weight, can be established by anyone who understands how to take a measurement. But it is the interpretation of data with respect to issues like cosmology that is important. The natural sciences are not only concerned with matters like weight, and it would be unfair to reduce them to this—something which seems to be the lowest part of their investigation.[24] Equally unfair would be to argue that the difference is so substantial that not even these sorts of studies (meas-urement) are in common.[25] Kuyper gave to perception an absolute character that transcends a person's worldview.[26] Such objects of knowledge are knowable by all humans at all times, but they hardly seem to be that for which humanity is inexcusable before God. In allowing for a common area of knowledge, Kuyper gave some credence to Reid's view, and hence to Princeton: "it should be grate-fully acknowledged that in the elementary parts of these studies there is a *com-mon* realm, in which the difference between view and starting-point does not enforce itself."[27]

It is the same with logic itself. Kuyper recognized that there is only one log-ic and not two different kinds of logic.[28] Hence there is some room for arguing that the unbelievers are not really following the "right reason." Involved in their unbelief is the denial of this logic that is not two, but one. But Kuyper used "log-ic" in a way that involves only inference between propositions. Thus logic can-not establish first principles in the way that reason (as the laws of thought) can. Logic only operates once there is a proposition from which to make a deduction. For Kuyper the two worldviews are contradictions. The naturalism of fallen man stands in contrast to the regenerate man who accepts special revelation from God, the Creator of the natural order. A person can be interested in science without being interested in studying the most fundamental principles of life. Kuyper saw that there are many aspects of science where details are studied, and awards can be won, without getting to the antithesis of the two worldviews. However, as this work is done, it brings out more clearly the antithesis of the two worldviews.[29]

There is a similarity here between Kuyper and Plato's allegory of the cave (*Republic* 7.514). In this allegory the prisoner who escapes the cave and views things as they are is taken to be insane by those still in the cave. But the cave dwellers make this accusation because they have not used reason to understand the nature of things (represented in the allegory as the sun which illuminates the world). The prisoners in the cave do not know about the world as it is, only about the reflections and their inductions based on these. Kuyper's division within humanity is similar. The unbelievers have the capacity to understand how things are. The difference between the believers and unbelievers is a difference of attitude with respect to the use of reason. One has used reason, although he had to be given the desire to do so by God through regeneration; the other has not been regenerated and does not want to use reason. Thus there is a standard for objective knowledge and science, and the generic science follows this stan-dard. Science, as Kuyper maintained, ought to follow some specific guidelines: He first assigned to investigate the nature and essence of God's revelation; sec-ond to analyze the material inferred from this; and third to explain how this ma-terial, including the revelation itself, relates to the intellectual life of man.[30]

Kuyper's two kinds of men form two kinds of theory. These are, roughly, the believer's worldview and the unbeliever's worldview. Kuyper further identi-fied them as the Christian and the Modern views: "But, in deadly opposition to this Christian element, against the very Christian name, and against its salutiferous influence in every sphere of life, the storm of Modernism has now arisen with violent intensity."[31] According to Kuyper these two worldviews are at odds with one another. Both cannot be true, and both cannot be false. Notice the use here of the law of non-contradiction. This is almost not worth mentioning because of its universal application in such situations. It seems that Kuyper is unaware of his reliance on reason, and this makes his claim that there is nothing that both the believer and unbeliever must commonly accept in order to build a worldview, doubtful.

Modernity and Christianity

The Modern worldview attacks Christianity and neither is reconcilable to the other. Kuyper saw this as a serious danger that imperiled Christianity. These two worldviews are wrestling with each other and are in mortal combat. He defined Modernism as essentially naturalism, the view that only the material world exists and all knowledge must be derived from the material world. On the other hand, the Christian worldview recognizes God as the Creator of the material world and sees the need for redemption through Christ.[32] The difference between the worldviews is a metaphysical difference. The Modern worldview looks to the then-contemporary German pantheism that tried to locate the eternal in the material universe itself.[33] In doing this, God is reduced to the universe as a whole, and stripped of his title as Creator. Hence such a position is in no way compatible with Christian theism, although part of the Modernist view is to try to reduce Christian Theism to naturalism. For Kuyper it was Protestantism alone that stood against the then-prevailing views of Pantheism that he attributed to an ascendancy in German Philosophy and as responsible for the evolutionary theory of Darwin.[34] Such a worldview is in direct opposition to Christianity, and seeks to replace it with a "hopeless modern Buddhism."[35]

Notice that Kuyper locates only one worldview that stands in contrast to Christianity: the Modern, or materialist, worldview. This worldview is monistic in character, and attempts to reduce all being to matter. In contrast, it seems fair to say of Hinduism that while it is monist, it attempts to reduce all being to self. Earlier, there were outlined three non-theistic worldviews, titled material monism, spiritual monism, and dualism. Kuyper did not deal with these last two, and his thinking on the issue seemed to be that if material monism was shown false then theism is true. However, there are other options beyond these two (Van Til makes the same mistake as will be seen below).

Calvinism as a Worldview

The Stone Lectures that Kuyper gave at Princeton in 1898 focused on Calvinism as a viable world and life view. The important point for Kuyper was to show first that Calvinism has all the characteristics of a world and life view, and second that it is a coherent world and life view. The importance of coherence rests on the importance given to the law of non-contradiction. If this law were avoidable, or jettisoned, coherence would lose all meaning. Kuyper's reliance on coherence, which to some extent is the method of proof for the correct world-view, demonstrates his need for this law, although it may not be a conscious part of his system. Kuyper's view of Calvinism is that it fulfills all the necessary conditions for a worldview. He placed it next to such "general systems of life" as Paganism, Islam, Roman Catholicism, and Modernism, in an attempt to show that Calvinism fulfills all the same conditions as these.[36] Further he argued that these conditions demand an explanation of the three fundamental relations of all human life; our relation to God, to man, and to the world.[37]

What makes Calvinism stand out is that it affirms that God is both transcendent and immanent. Only God is without beginning, and all else was made by God. In contrast, the other worldviews try to find the eternal in some aspect of the creation. Kuyper contrasted Calvinism with Paganism, Roman Catholicism, and Islam. He believed that Paganism seeks God in the creation, Roman Catholicism posits a mediate communion between humanity and God, and Islam isolates God from the creation. Calvinism, however, is based on the claim that while God is the creator, God also enters into the creation in order to have immediate (as opposed to mediate) fellowship with humanity.[38] It is the relationship of the creation to the Creator that is the defining point of every worldview. And Calvinism stands out as unique in this respect. This is what was pointed out above in contrast to material monism, spiritual monism, and dualism. It is theism that claims only God is eternal. And within theism Kuyper argued that only Calvinism consistently develops the view of God.

Kuyper, Inexcusability and Clarity

However, Kuyper's view does not seem to preserve the relationship between inexcusability and clarity. If there is not a clear general revelation of God, then it appears problematic for humanity to be held accountable for its failure to know God. Kuyper does affirm that there is a knowledge of God through general revelation (natural theology), but in a much different way than Warfield. Kuyper argued that "Natural theology is with us no schema, but the knowledge of God itself, which still remains in the sinner and is still within his reach, entirely in harmony with the sense of Rom. i 19 *sq.* and Rom. ii 14 *sq.*"[39] There is a knowledge of God that the sinner both possesses and denies that he possesses. There is a common grace that allows the sinner to exercise some of his capacity to know. But even this common grace reveals God in that if reason were properly used the sinner would see his need for God.[40] Kuyper argued that even with the reality of sin there is a spark of light. Usually such metaphors (light) are used to explain reason, and so it seems fair to say that the unbeliever is left some use of reason. Even in the fallen state, humans, if they used reason properly, could know God. If true, this means that the problem is not with reason, but with the sinner.

Thus, for Kuyper, God's nature can be known through creation. Sin has dimmed man's ability to know, but not completely. What this means is central to this study. Unfortunately, it is ambiguous. How can reason be dimmed? It seems that either reason reveals God or it does not. And does this revelation get through? Does the sinner know God, and yet not know God? What does it mean to know God? Answering these questions will be important not only for Kuyper, but also for Van Til later in the study. Perhaps, it is the ambiguity here that causes the problems Warfield sees. Whatever the case, Kuyper's argument has the air of circularity about it: Kuyper stated there are two worldviews; he further said that these worldviews are contradictions of each other, and all reasoning by any person is relative to his first principles. This means that each worldview will reject the conclusions of the other worldview; however, this means that Kuyper's theory about there being two worldviews is relative to his worldview—most likely his opponents in the other worldview would not accept his view. How did Kuyper arrive at his conclusion? Did he do it in a way that is demonstrable to others in the contradictory worldview? If his claim that both worldviews cannot be true is based on the law of non-contradiction, is this a law of thought that the unbelievers would accept? Is the law of non-contradiction a "neutral" law that both sides can agree to? If so, Warfield's claim about right reason makes a good deal of sense. The difference between the two worldviews is a difference in the consistent use of reason. Reason, used properly, leads to only one worldview. The fallen man has beliefs that are ultimately contradictory to reason itself. Kuyper addressed this claim of circularity head on when he said:

> If the objection be raised that in the prosecution of science as directed by palingenesis, it is a matter of pre-assumption that there is a God, that a creation took place, that sin reigns, etc., we grant this readily, but in the same sense in which it is pre-assumed in all science that there is a human being, that human beings think, that it is possible for this human being to think mistakenly, etc., etc. He to whom these last-named things are not presuppositions, will not so much as put his hand to the plough in the field of science; and such is the case with him who does not know, with greater certainty than he knows his own existence, that God is his Creator.[41]

But what does Kuyper's view do for clarity? If it is clear that only one worldview is coherent, then to what extent are there really two worldviews? The difference is a difference with respect to the use of reason. One first principle is self-contradictory, the other is not. But Kuyper wanted "God" to be posited as a first principle in the way that the "common sense" ideas were for Reid. God makes argumentation possible, and should not be held up to "human standards" (including reason) by men. Kuyper saw this as a kind of reverence.[42] For a theologian to put himself in the place to investigate God is a reversal of the order. The result of this is that the theologian who takes this approach either reverses the order of things and places the theologian as the critic of God, or falsifies the object of study and in the place of God puts religious phenomena. This second result might appear more innocent than the first, but Kuyper asserted that it results in a lack of the knowledge of God, which is essentially intellectual atheism.[43] This change in the focus of theology may have been a result of the Kantian influence. Kant argued that reason cannot know God, but rather that God must be postulated as a basis for morality. This means either that theology cannot be pursued as a science which uses reason to study God, or that the object of theology must be changed from God to something that can be known through reason such as religious experience or social history.

Kuyper and Knowing God

Even if there had been no sin to deter humanity in their seeking of God, Kuyper claimed that God's existence would not have been a matter of the believer's empirical investigations. Such investigations presuppose a worldview in which they are being interpreted. Thus, it is in theism that empirical investigations make sense. They cannot then be used to prove the theism that gave them their meaning. Kuyper believed that the knowledge of God must be imparted actively by God to the knower. This would be true even had there been no sin. But with the reality of sin, humanity is not even able to receive the knowledge passively. God must change the human attitude, or "heart." In the sinful state, humanity cannot come to know God without redemption given by God. This means that either the sinner will live without knowing God, or God must act to restore the sinner through redemption. This act of God is necessary in order to bring a sinner to the knowledge of God.[44] There is a temptation to claim that the clarity of general revelation is diminished due to sin. Kuyper may have said something like this. But the objective reality that reason reveals God does not change due to sin; rather sin is the failure to use reason to know God. Thus, it can be maintained both that general revelation is clear, and that humans as sinners do not see what should be seen. To affirm that general revelation is clear is not to affirm that sinners can achieve redemption apart from special revelation. Kuyper believed that sinners cannot come to know God apart from God acting in the sinners' lives, however he does not appear to affirm that general revelation is clear even after the Fall, and this may be part of the reason he diminishes the role of apologetics.

One important aspect of Kuyper's theology to keep in mind is his view of the goal of the Christian life. If the Holy Spirit regenerates the elect so that they can go to heaven, there is little need for reason and proofs. These are at best a nicety in that they show that Christianity is not an absurdity, and comfort can be derived from this. But they are not necessary. But what if the goal of the Christian life is knowing God, and this understanding can only be attained by seeking? Seeking involves a process of seeing what is basic, and of distinguishing between "a" and "non-a," or "eternal" and "non-eternal." In making this distinction the seeker also comes to understand that what is eternal created what is not eternal, and that there is a clear distinction between these so that any failure to make this distinction is inexcusable.

This is consistent with the role of the Holy Spirit as understood by Kuyper. The Holy Spirit regenerates, or restores a sinner to life. This restoration is a return to seeking, understanding, and doing what is right. Thus, one who is regenerated all the more should be able to show what is clear. Regeneration does not get one out of the requirement to seek and understand, but restores one to the ability to do so. The reluctance to seek and understand, and instead insist that these are not necessary to go to heaven, reveals that there is not a fear of failing to know God. The fear of failing to know God and the consequences that come into life when joy is not found in knowing God, are the only motivations that can get a person to seek. Without these, it should not be expected that a person will seek, and without seeking it is not possible to understand.

Redemption and Special Revelation

The Christian claims that the sinner must be redeemed by God. The mind must be renewed by the power of God. Warfield agreed with this. But what does this mean with respect to clarity? Once dead in sin humanity does not care to know God and must be born again. But the state of being dead in sin is due to a failure to see what is clear in the first place. Hence, the continued state of death is a continued state of failure to see what is clear. And being "born again" is being returned back to the state of seeing what is clear about God. This does not seem to come out in Kuyper's view. Clarity has little place, and it seems hard to locate at best. This was Warfield's complaint, as will be seen below.[45] While the work of the Holy Spirit is necessary for rebirth, it is not necessary for the responsibility to believe in God.

But before Warfield's critique of Kuyper is examined, it is necessary to understand the role of special revelation in Kuyper's theory. For Kuyper, and later for Van Til, there is no possibility of knowledge apart from special revelation (Kantian influence). Kuyper argued that the indispensability of the scriptures rests on two conditions: first, the necessity of the special principle given the weakening of the natural principle; second, that this special principle does not work atomistically to one individual, but to the whole human race (hence it is in written form).[46]

Kuyper developed the need for Scripture in a way that claims sin darkens man's understanding and leaves him without the ability to know. No knowledge of God is possible for fallen man apart from the scriptures. The reality of sin is that no one is seeking God, and in this condition no one will know God. Thus without special revelation it is not possible for a person in the state of sin to know God.[47]

There are subtle nuances in this that must be handled with care. Warfield agreed that apart from regeneration none seek, none understand, and none do what is right. Regeneration is necessary for fallen man to come to know God. This regeneration accompanies the preaching of the Gospel found in the scriptures. Yet, humanity is inexcusable precisely because, if people used reason, they could know God. "While reiterating the teaching of nature as to the existence and character of the personal Creator and Lord of all, the scriptures lay their stress upon the grace or the undeserved love of God, as exhibited in His dealings with His sinful and wrath-deserving creatures."[48] The knowledge of God is available through general revelation, and the human failure to posses this knowledge leaves them in a miserable state before the justice of God.[49] This failure is sin. Humanity has a responsibility to believe in God apart from the work of the Holy Spirit. This difference provides a clear distinction between Kuyper and Warfield, and then, later, with Van Til as he argued against what he perceived to be weaknesses in Warfield.

Warfield and Kuyper

The difference between Warfield and Kuyper is not a difference with respect to effectual calling. Both agree that life is given only by the Holy Spirit. Instead it is an epistemological difference. Kuyper was more of a coherentist, while Warfield, following Scottish Common Sense Philosophy, was a foundationalist. Warfield's position was not that a person in the state of sin can come to know God through the work of apologetics. He affirmed that only through the redemptive work of God can the person who is dead in sin be brought to life in knowing God. However, he argued that faith is a form of conviction and is therefore grounded in evidence, and that evidence has its part to play in the conversion of the soul. Apologetics operates as an ordinary means both in the conversion of the individual and in the interaction between Christianity and non-Christian worldviews.[50] For Warfield, this was not a small part, nor was it a secondary or merely defensive part. He rejected the idea that its sole purpose was to protect Christians from the surrounding world, or to help the distracted Christian bring his intellect into conformity with his heart. Instead, Warfield saw the part that apologetics has to play as a central part in spreading the Gospel to the world and in addressing the challenges of non-Christian worldviews.[51] This implies that it is the duty of a Christian to use reason. As was noted above, Charles Hodge saw the fundamental job of reason as avoiding contradictions. Reason as the law of non-contradiction stands as judge over statements and systems. Where there is a contradiction, there cannot be truth (or meaning). This, for Warfield, was the distinction of Christianity. He believed that only Christianity can reason its way to dominion.[52] It is in this way that Christianity stands out from all other religions. It need not appeal to the sword, or seek some other way to extend itself. This means that the Christian has a duty to use reason.

With that in mind, Warfield and Kuyper differ dramatically with respect to apologetics. The two kinds of men, and the resulting two kinds of science, that Kuyper spoke of are not completely rejected by Warfield. It seems essential to Christianity that there are believers and unbelievers, and that these two differ with respect to their worldviews. But what was rejected by Warfield is that there are two reasons, or two methods for knowing, that both result in a science. For Warfield the two sciences differ with respect to how consistent they are; they do not differ in kind. "There certainly do exist these 'two kinds of men' in the world—men under the unbroken sway of sin, and men who have been brought under the power of the palingenesis [regeneration]. And the produce of the in-

vestigation of these 'two kinds of men' will certainly give us 'two kinds of science'."[53] But Warfield insisted that this difference is not really a difference in
kind, but is more a matter of corruption. "The depraved man neither thinks, nor
feels, nor wills as he ought; and the products of his actions as a scientific thinker
cannot possibly escape the influence of this everywhere operative destructive
power."[54] Warfield argued with Kuyper in pointing out that the different sciences
are affected in different degrees depending on the objects of their study.[55]

Rationality and Christianity

For Warfield, the Christian worldview is the only rational worldview. All
others reject reason at some basic point. A belief is basic to a worldview in that
it explains that worldview's belief about what "being" is independent/eternal,
and what "being" is dependent/temporal. If God as the Creator is denied this
status, and some aspect of the universe (or the universe in its entirety) is viewed
as eternal, then knowledge in others areas is not possible. "Without the knowledge of God it is not too much to say we know nothing rightly, so that the renunciation of the knowledge of God carries with it renunciation of all right
knowledge."[56] Reason must be used consistently if it is to be used at all.[57] And
this is the absurdity, rationally speaking, of the unbeliever's position. The unbeliever is being inconsistent at almost every point, and yet often times is claiming
loudly to be using reason. Warfield argued that Christianity is not one of two
worldviews, but the only worldview that is rational:

> We believe in Christ because it is rational to believe in him, not though it be ir-
> rational. Accordingly, our Reformed fathers always posited in the production of
> faith the presence of the 'argumentum propter quod credo,' as well as the
> 'principium seu causa efficiens a quo ad credendum adducor.' That is to say,
> for the birth of faith in the soul, it is just as essential that grounds of faith
> should be present to the mind as that the Giver of faith should act creatively
> upon the heart.[58]

The distinguishing mark of the Christian worldview is that the believer is
able to know God as God has revealed Himself. This includes a knowledge from
general revelation, and the use of reason itself to understand all revelation. The
difference between the two worldviews is not a difference (or not only) with
respect to special revelation. Kuyper gave apologetics a very small role because
he thought reason cannot take the place of the Holy Spirit in giving new life.
Warfield agreed about the Holy Spirit, but saw that there is a responsibility to
know God apart from the work of the Holy Spirit, and the role of reason is one
of the ordinary means that the Holy Spirit uses. Reason must be used even to
understand the scriptures, which are authoritative for the believer. In this Warfield differed dramatically from Kuyper and Van Til. He argued that while it is
true that a Christian must take his stand in the scriptures, he must first have these
scriptures authenticated to him as such.[59] It is fair to ask which books really are

scriptures and which are not. Similarly, it is also true to say that Christianity is attained not by evidences and arguments but by a new birth.[60] It is not within the power of arguments to make a Christian.[61] "Paul may plant, and Apollos water; it is God alone who gives the increase."[62] It does not follow, however, that Paul should stop planting and Apollos stop watering. "Faith is the gift of God; but it does not in the least follow that the faith that God gives is an irrational faith, that is, a faith without grounds in right reason."[63]

Thus there is a "common ground" that the believer can point to in speaking with the unbeliever. If knowledge is desired, this common ground cannot be denied. Taken as the laws of thought, reason is the common ground. Reason is not neutral in that it certainly reveals that there is a Creator. But reason is common in that all thinkers use it to some extent. In order to form a concept and express it in a word one must use the law of identity. Apart from this no word would be intelligible (Hodge gave the job of grasping meaning to reason). This means that there is only one body of knowledge, called science. This body of knowledge can be contributed to by the sinful human, although that contribution will not be what it could have been apart from sin. Warfield affirmed that the scientific work of the sinful human contributes a substantive part to the abstract science produced by what he called the ideal subject, although it is less valuable than it would have been without sin.[64]

Reason and Apologetics

Warfield believed that it is the use of reason with respect to the only reasonable worldview that apologetics is concerned with. And apologetics can fulfill this function. He affirmed that the believer can show the unbeliever that the non-Christian worldview, first principles and all, is fundamentally inconsistent. At this point the unbeliever has only the option of giving up his worldview or giving up reason. For Warfield this gave a very important function to apologetics. Apologetics is not concerned with addressing how this particular argument or person can be induced to become a Christian.[65] It is concerned with something much more fundamental. It concerns itself with the actual establishment, "after a fashion valid for all normally working minds and for all ages of the world in its developing thought" of the basic facts that constitute Christianity.[66] Notice that "all normally working minds" sounds very similar to Reid, and reflects the influence of Scottish Common Sense Philosophy. The idea of "all normally working minds" is not that a poll be taken of all people to decide how people in fact try to get knowledge (mistakenly or otherwise). The idea is that there are some basic and necessary prerequisites for knowing, called reason, that are available to all men at all times. These can be used to establish the true system that, in virtue of being true, all men ought to believe. This gives to all the ability to know the Christian worldview, in a fundamental sense.

Warfield found the misapprehension of apologetics in a common duality among theologians, the antinomies of rationalism and mysticism. For Warfield the first is the attempt to find all knowledge through reason. This is rationalism.

It claims to use reason and yet does not use reason fully because it fails to examine its assumptions. Rationalism denies the need for special revelation. The mystic, on the other hand, denies to reason any ability to gain knowledge. For the mystic, experience of the divine (usually a very ambiguous event) is the source of knowledge. For the mystic, reason is unable to arrive at a knowledge of the divine. Hence: "To Rationalism, of course, Apologetics were an inanity; to Mysticism, an impertinence."[67] Wherever rationalism has been presupposed, there is proportionally a questioning of the validity of apologetics. And wherever mysticism has been presupposed, the use of apologetics is questioned and in general apologetics is distrusted.[68]

During Warfield's time, and most likely during the present as well, the rationalist principle was the most common. "At the present moment, the Rationalistic tendency is perhaps most active . . . where religion is supposed to seek and find expression only in value-judgments—the subjective product of the human soul in its struggle after personal freedom—and thus to stand out of all relation with theoretical knowledge, there, obviously, there is no place for a vindication of Christian faith to reason and no possibility of Apologetics."[69] Rationalism seeks coherence while working within the fallen principles. This is not the same as the use of reason to know God. Rationalism assumes principles that are at the outset self-contradictory (those of the natural man), and then deduces from these conclusions that are contradictory to the Christian world and life view. An example is Modernism and its cosmology of evolution. It assumes that matter can account for itself without reference to a Creator. Beginning with this assumption, it uses reason as a deductive method to draw out implications. These implications are consistent with its assumptions, but those assumptions may themselves be contrary to reason. Thus, a fault of rationalism is that it does not use reason fully enough. It uses reason constructively by building on assumptions, but does not use it critically to examine those assumptions.

This misuse of reason leads many, like Kuyper, to abandon reason altogether.

> The mystical tendency is showing itself in our day most markedly in a widespread inclination to decline Apologetics in favor or the so-called *testimonium Spiritus Sancti*. The convictions of the Christian man, we are told, are not the product of reasons addressed to his intellect, but are the immediate creation of the Holy Spirit in his heart. Therefore, it is intimated, we can not only do very well without these reasons, but it is something very like sacrilege to attend to them. Apologetics, accordingly, is not merely useless, but may even become noxious, because tending to substitute a barren intellectualism for a vital faith.[70]

In this view one will become committed by experiencing for himself that the worldview in question is beneficial. Of course, this is problematic because what counts as "beneficial" depends on a person's worldview. This (Kuyper's view of apologetics) was Warfield's main complaint against Kuyper. Apologetics was not abolished altogether by Kuyper, but it was given a subordinate role, as a subdivision of a subdivision of the "Dogmatological Group" where it is given the task of defending Christianity from philosophy (narrowly defined).[71] For all of the other significant contributions that Kuyper made, his view of reason, and consequently apologetics, left Christianity as the great assumption. Why pick Christianity over another view? Warfield believed that those who follow Kuyper's thinking will say that one should pick it because they have experienced that it is good. They have tried it out for themselves (in a manner of speaking) and seen that it works.[72]

Kuyper's role for apologetics was not to abolish it, but to give it a job of little importance. This follows from Kuyper's view of reason. Reason is incompetent with respect to convincing others. The two worldviews produce two kinds of men that cannot speak to each other about first principles. Warfield argued against Kuyper by vindicating reason itself. While the scriptures are the source of theology, they themselves must be understood by reason. Reason helps a person to understand what the scriptures are, and what they mean. Hence, to posit them as a first principle is incorrect. Reason can be used to show that God exists, and it is used to understand God's special revelation with respect to redemption. This point about reason is the basic difference between Warfield and Kuyper. Warfield admitted that there are many attractive aspects to Kuyper's development of the theological sciences.[73] However, he saw it as a mistake to make the scriptures the basic principle of knowledge.[74] Warfield argued that the scriptures are not the object of theology, but its source.[75] Its object being the knowledge of God, and this must be shown to be in the scriptures. However, before this can happen, it must be shown that there is a knowledge of God in the world, and previous to this is that there is a knowledge of God possible to man.[76] And before this, it must be shown that there is a God to know, and with this line of thought Warfield argued that it is necessary to argue back to first principles.[77] These first principles are the realm of an apologetical theology, and this of necessity stands in the first place among the essential theological disciplines.[78] Because knowing God is the highest use of the human mind, and it is fundamental to all of life, any attempt to do science apart from God will be fatally incomplete.[79] The role Kuyper assigned to reason cannot be understood apart from his view of knowledge itself. Because Warfield and Kuyper differed with respect to knowledge, it comes as no surprise that they differ with respect to the role of apologetics.

Conclusion

Warfield's position with respect to reason and consequently apologetics is made clearer by contrasting it with Kuyper's. Kuyper's worldview relativism correctly pointed out the importance of first principles to a system. Warfield did not disagree with this. Kuyper also pointed out that these systems produce conclusions that are relative to their first principles. Again, Warfield agreed. However, Kuyper's view makes it impossible to judge between first principles. To some extent this is a defect in Reid's philosophy. It must be established, of each "common sense principle," that argumentation really is impossible if the principle were violated. The failure to do this is one contributing factor in the Common Sense Philosophy losing popularity. This loss in popularity is most likely due to the fideistic tendencies of Common Sense Philosophy.

However, if reason is defined narrowly as Charles Hodge mentioned above, are there really two reasonable first principles (theism vs. naturalism)? Are not the modernist's first principles self-contradictory? If so, the problem is with the use of reason. The correct use of reason at the basic level reveals that God is the Creator of the heavens and the earth and is owed whatsoever worship He desires from men. This approach states that humanity can use reason to know God, and can use reason to know that the opposite of the belief in God is self-contradictory (not possible).[80]

From here it makes sense to turn to Warfield's legacy. Specific attention will be given to Cornelius Van Til who accepted a position at Princeton in the years following Warfield's death, and was among the founding professors at Westminster Theological Seminary. Van Til is chosen because he was the shaping influence in apologetics at Westminster, and because he consciously tried to find a third position between Warfield and Kuyper. Many of Van Til's criticisms of Warfield revolved around the idea that reason cannot be used to judge God, and hence it is necessary to keep in mind Warfield's view of reason while proceeding.

Questions:
1. What are the worldviews that Kuyper identifies and how do they differ?
2. If worldviews have incommensurable starting points, on what basis does Kuyper believe humans can interact?
3. How does Kuyper's view of regeneration and going to heaven minimize the need for seeking and understanding?
4. Why is the regenerate person all the more responsible to seek and understand?
5. What is the only motivation that can be expected to produce seeking to know God?
6. What role does Kuyper assign to apologetics?
7. What is Warfield's view of "reason"?
8. For Warfield, what is the purpose of reason and apologetics if it is the Holy Spirit that regenerates?

CHAPTER 5:
CORNELIUS VAN TIL AND PRESUPPOSITIONS

The challenges of Modernity to Christian doctrines about the origin and nature of man, source of authority and knowledge, and role of redemption in human society, required a response. The failure of Christians to find a unified response led to divisions such as that found at Princeton Theological Seminary. Can Christians find a response that preserves the meaning of the message of redemption? Or has Modernity shown that Christianity is making declarations without proof?

B.B. Warfield's legacy is not simple, nor does the following purport to make it seem that way. However, because Westminster Theological Seminary explicitly claimed to continue the tradition of the Old School Princeton Theology it makes sense to look there for a continuation of Warfield's method. And, because the present focus is on apologetics, it makes sense to look at Cornelius Van Til who taught at Princeton Theological, was one of the founding professors at Westminster, and who developed the apologetical system, known as "Presuppositional Apologetics," that characterizes this seminary. While Van Til tried to avoid what he saw as mistakes in both Warfield and Kuyper, he replaced reason with special revelation, and did not explain clarity in a way to maintain inexcusability. Therefore, it will be argued that Van Til departed enough from Warfield's concept of "right reason" to do harm to the attempt of the apologist to show the inexcusability of all unbelief.

The Split at Princeton

The changes at Princeton Theological Seminary and the beginning of Westminster Theological and the Orthodox Presbyterian Church revolved largely around J. Gresham Machen (1881–1937). It was Machen's concern for consistency with respect to the historic Church that led him and others to leave Princeton. Of this, W. Stanford Reid said:

Although in 1926 the Directors wanted him [J. Gresham Machen] to become professor of apologetics, a move to which he was not much inclined, the Trustees, led by the president, J. Ross Stevenson, were opposed. The result was a battle that led to the reorganization of the administration: the Board of Directors was abolished and full control of the school was given to a single Board of Trustees to which two signers of the liberal Auburn Affirmation were appointed. The resulting conflict between Machen and the new administration led to his resignation from the seminary in June 1929, on the ground that Princeton had now left its historic theological position.[1]

It was in this context that Westminster Theological was established, as an attempt to preserve what Princeton had been. When Machen left Princeton, a number of others also did who agreed that the historic creeds of the faith summed up true Christian doctrine and should not be departed from in favor of what Machen and others viewed to be compromises with non-Christian worldviews. When Machen left, others also decided to leave. As a result they formed a committee to establish a new seminary named Westminster, located in Philadelphia, as an independent institution in the fall of 1929. In his opening address at Westminster Theological Seminary, Machen emphasized two aspects of its constitution. The first was the final authority of the Bible, which he said should be read as meaning exactly what it says. The second was that Princeton was lost to the cause of evangelicalism, and that Westminster would stand firmly in the Reformed theological position as expressed in the Westminster Confession of Faith.[2]

Van Til's Alternative to Warfield and Kuyper

Because of Van Til's presence at Princeton, and his role at Westminster, his view is important for this work. Particularly of concern is his view of apologetics and how it represented both the Princeton tradition, and Warfield particularly, as well as Kuyper's position. Van Til attempted to formulate a third position that takes the best of both of these, and yet avoids what he saw as weaknesses in each. Some, like R.C. Sproul, accuse Van Til of being a Kuyperian (see Sproul's *Classical Apologetics*). But students of Van Til, like Greg Bahnsen, deny this and point to explicit statements by Van Til to the contrary (see Bahnsen's *Van Til's Apologetics: Reading and Analysis*).[3] Here the concern is not with settling this matter so much as it is with understanding Van Til's epistemology and its affect on his system of apologetics. Van Til relied heavily on the notion of a transcendental reason expounded by Kant. This had a defining affect on his system.

Van Til defined apologetics as: "the vindication of the Christian philosophy of life against the various forms of the non-Christian philosophy of life."[4] Like Warfield, Van Til saw the crux of apologetics in the proof of the theistic God's existence. He contrasted this with the "evidences" that are used to prove other truths of Christianity. Although Van Til's system is presuppositional, in contrast to evidential, he did not deny that evidences have a place in proof. Van Til distinguished between apologetics as giving proofs for theism, and evidences giving proofs for Christianity.[5] That is, apologetics deals with philosophy while evidences deal with facts.[6] And because apologetics deals with philosophy, specifically with establishing the foundation, it also deals with how evidences are to be interpreted. The interpretation of a given "evidence" is an essential part for that evidence playing a role in an argument or proof. Evidences by themselves are not enough to prove Christianity. Evidences must be interpreted to be meaningful, and hence what a specific "fact" means will depend on one's world and life view. Van Til gave an example of this:

> It is impossible and useless to seek to vindicate Christianity as a historical religion by a discussion of facts only. Suppose we assert that Christ arose from the grave. We assert further that his resurrection proves his divinity. This is the nerve of the 'historical argument' for Christianity. Yet a pragmatic philosopher will refuse to follow this line of reasoning. Granted he allows that Christ actually arose from the grave, he will say that this proves nothing more than that something very unusual took place in the case of 'that man Jesus.' The philosophy of the pragmatist is to the effect that everything in this universe is unrelated and that such a fact as the resurrection of Jesus, granted it were a fact, would have no significance for us who live two thousand years after him. It is apparent from this that if we would really defend Christianity as an historical religion we must at the same time defend the theism upon which Christianity is based. This involves us in philosophical discussion.[7]

The aim of apologetics is to demonstrate the truth of theism while showing that all other worldviews are false. Of course this is not derived exclusively from either Warfield or Kuyper since both saw apologetics as having this goal. The work of both Charles Hodge and A.A. Hodge included sections demonstrating the inconsistency of all non-theistic worldviews. And this certainly does seem to be the general aim of apologetics. Hence, it is no surprise when Greg Bahnsen said of Van Til that the latter viewed apologetics as the defense of the Christian faith by answering all the variety of challenges brought against it by unbelievers.[8] The Christian apologist establishes Christianity as the true worldview, over and against all non-Christian philosophies of life.[9] This is certainly in-line with the Princeton approach, as well as Kuyper's approach.

Van Til's Epistemology

The uniqueness of Van Til appears when consideration is given to his epistemology. In this he did differ to some extent from Warfield and Kuyper, at least in his reliance on Kant. What Kant called a Copernican revolution in philosophy, Van Til called a Copernican revolution in apologetics. The revolution deals with a change from attempting to conform the mind to the world, to realizing that the world must conform to the mind. There are, for Kant, *a priori* principles through which all information is interpreted by the mind.[10] Hence, there is no way to "get at" the world apart from these. All that is available is the data once it has gone through the formal structure of the mind. In a way, this is to say that there are necessary preconditions for knowing, reasoning, and argumentation (as was seen in Reid earlier). Interestingly, for nineteenth century positivism, Kant's Copernican revolution entailed that "metaphysical views are no longer tenable."[11] This reliance on Kant has been traced to the Dutch Reformed tradition. Donald Fuller and Richard Gardiner argue, "it was the Dutch Neo-Calvinist Abraham Kuyper (as well as the Neo-orthodox generally) who, in fact, yielded to 'Enlightenment' views of metaphysics, science, and theology. It is our contention that while Old Princeton maintained and championed a pre-Kantian theological method, the Dutch Neo-Calvinist theologians reshaped Reformed theology to fit the mold of the Kantian worldview and a distinctively modern philosophy of science."[12]

The Presuppositions of Worldviews

Greg Bahnsen claimed that this presuppositional approach is one of the most important contributions given by Van Til. "One of the distinctive insights that Van Til has given to presuppositional apologetics is that every line of reasoning that is exalted against the knowledge of God, and every kind of objection or challenge to the faith that is raised by unbelievers, arises from an attitude of the heart and within the intellectual context of a world-and-life view."[13] Rather than argue against evolution *per se*, or against Marx's view of history, or Freud's view of man, the apologist must argue against the atheism/naturalism that are behind these. Each of these thinkers (Darwin, Marx, and Freud) assume naturalism, and assume that the Christian view is incorrect. Hence, they are not as "objective" or "neutral", as they would like to appear, but are very much saturated with assumptions that lead necessarily to the conclusions they draw. They may be internally consistent, but the question becomes whether their first principles, their presuppositions, are coherent. The presuppositions of a worldview affect every other part of the worldview, and consequently the entire outlook of the person. It is because of this that every encounter between worldviews is ultimately a conflict between their presuppositions. Thus, every apologetical encounter is a conflict between conflicting worldviews.[14]

Van Til, like Kuyper, located a basic non-Christian principle that is behind the fallen world and life view. This principle places humans as the source of knowledge, and elevates human "reason" to the place where God is for the Christian. Here there will be some ambiguities that arise because the term "reason" is sometimes used to refer to what are clearly the non-Christian naturalistic assumptions, which are by no means self-evidently true. At other times a method much like Charles Hodge's will be used in terms of reason as the law of non-contradiction. So Van Til's denial of the fallen man's ability to achieve knowledge through his own "reason" seems best defined not as the law of non-contradiction, but as a deductive/inductive method based on naturalism that produces such cosmologies as evolution and the oscillating universe theory. These are relative to their naturalist assumptions and hence cannot be true if naturalism is not true. In terms of his reliance of first principles, Van Til bears similarity to Kuyper. Van Til also affirmed that the most basic assumption of the non-Christian worldview is that humanity, rather than God, is the final reference point in predication. Van Til thought that the idea of truth, as an abstract entity, disconnected it from God, and was therefore based on the non-Christian assumption.[15] For Van Til this meant that there can be no neutral place, or common ground, between the Christian and non-Christian. Whether a neutral place and common ground are to be equated was not questioned.

Van Til located the fallen human's assumptions as essentially placing humanity at the center. It is the job of the Apologist to challenge this notion. Can such a starting point really end up in knowledge? Van Til argued that it cannot, and that this is what the Reformed Apologist must point out. The Reformed Apologist must challenge this starting point in everything that the unbeliever says about anything.[16] It is this assumption that the "natural man" uses to interpret everything that is presented to him. In this sense, it should be no wonder that the natural man rejects creation as an account of the origin of life. It is not because he is more "scientific" than the believer. It is because the natural man is confined to look for the cause of what he sees in the material world itself, rather than in the Creator of that world. This approach to apologetics tests basic beliefs for meaning.

Van Til called this method "presuppositional", and this name has come to characterize his apologetical system. In arguing presuppositionally the apologist locates and challenges the first principle, or most basic belief, on which the non-Christian view hinges. All views have presuppositions. "Everybody thinks and reasons in terms of a broad and fundamental understanding of the nature of reality, of how we know and of how we should live our lives."[17] This establishes how the apologist will approach argumentation against non-theistic worldviews. "To argue by presupposition is to indicate what are the epistemological and metaphysical principles that underlie and control one's method."[18] Van Til claimed that the presupposition for Christianity is the ontological Trinity, and this ultimately controls the Christian methodology.[19] The isolation of a system's basic assumption and the consequent evaluation of that assumption is not a unique characteristic of Van Til. What is important are the beliefs Van Til saw as being basic to a system.

The Transcendental Argument

The "transcendental argument" is another central feature to Van Til's apologetic. The argument is essentially that no arguments are possible apart from theism. It is only in the theistic worldview that argumentation makes sense. Van Til argued that the unbeliever cannot have any knowledge without being untrue to his presuppositions. It is only the theistic worldview that can consistently explain knowledge, science, morality, and everything else. Thus, it is either the case that the unbeliever does not know what he claims to know, or that the unbeliever does have knowledge but only because in this instance he is borrowing theistic principles to gain knowledge. If the unbeliever were consistent to his naturalism, knowledge would not be possible. The unbeliever tries to claim that logic, science, and morality are on his side against the Christian.[20] Van Til answered this by arguing that these are only possible within the Christian worldview, and only Christianity can rescue them from meaninglessness.[21] Van Til's challenge to the unbeliever was guided by the assumption that only Christianity provides the framework in which human reasoning and knowledge are possible.[22] This is called a "transcendental" defense of Christianity.[23] It is called "transcendental" because it argues for those principles necessary for any argumentation. Any attempt for a human to reason, and even reason and reasoning itself, are incoherent unless the truth of the Christian scriptures is assumed, or presupposed.[24]

Van Til and Reason

Van Til claimed that man's reasoning is unintelligible unless the Christian scriptures are presupposed. For the purposes here, this is important in terms of the definition of "reason", as well as for what it does to the clarity of general revelation. If "reason" is taken to be the contemporary popular assumptions, then such assumptions as these are cultural and conventional. Different people, in different places, at different times, claim to "know" statements that contradict each other. Widespread belief is by no means knowledge. That our culture takes for granted the truth of the theory of evolution does not make it true. Hence, to take one's stand in the "reason" of the day is specious "reasoning". But what if reason is taken in the sense that Hodge gave above? What if reason is the laws of thought, those laws necessary for thought itself? Hodge saw the law of non-contradiction as an obvious example. While Van Til argued that only Christian Theism can explain such a law, it seems he nevertheless used the law to argue for theism. His Transcendental Argument presupposes the law of non-contradiction: The non-Christian world and life view is false because it is self-contradictory, therefore Christianity is true. This is the law of non-contradiction being applied to basic beliefs. Therefore, it seems that the first assumption is that this law is necessary for thought, and only after that does one question which view is consistent.

What does this say for clarity? Van Til affirmed both general revelation, and the necessity of the scriptures for any knowledge. This is not the distinction that both Warfield and Kuyper made above with respect to the work of the Holy Spirit to renew men's hearts. Van Til agreed with them on that point. But his use of Scripture as the presupposition necessary for all knowledge is more than this; it is an epistemological claim about how to know, not an ontological claim about the ability to know. For Van Til the fall of man occurred when man tried to do without God in every part of life.[25] Humans sought the source of truth, goodness, and beauty in something besides God, either in self or in the material universe.

The result is that humans tried to establish a worldview in which they interpreted all data apart from reference to God. In contrast, Van Til argued that persons must take their ideas about the nature of reality from the Bible, it being the final standard of truth itself. This is different from Warfield in an important way. Remember that Warfield argued that the Bible must first be authenticated as special revelation. This means that for Warfield there is a standard for gaining knowledge more basic than the Bible itself.

Van Til affirmed the relation of redemptive revelation (supernatural revelation, or scriptures), and general revelation (natural revelation). He argued that special revelation is necessary because of the covenant disobedience on the part of Adam in Paradise.[26] Van Til saw the sin that caused humanity to fall as a violation of a positive supernatural revelation. That is, God spoke to Adam and told him not to eat of the Tree of the Knowledge of Good and Evil. What Van Til left unclear is how Adam knew it was God that told him this. How did Adam know God? Presumably one must first know God before one can know not to violate a command of God. It seems at least fair to assert that it was first a failure to know God as the Creator that allowed Adam to eat thus breaking God's command. This knowing God as Creator is what all humans are held accountable for. But Van Til's description of the Fall as only the breaking of a commandment leaves unclear exactly what humanity is accountable for.

If the above considerations are correct, it follows that humanity could know God apart from the Christian scriptures. Perhaps, aspects of God's justice, mercy, and redemption cannot be known and are properly the subject of redemptive revelation, but God's eternal power and divine nature can be known. And it follows that these can be known of God after the Fall through general revelation. Reason does not fall (as if the law of non-contradiction became false after the Fall), but rather the desire to use reason changed. Van Til maintained that these truths about God could be known even after the Fall.[27] "Grace can be recognized as grace only in contrast to God's curse on nature."[28] In this Van Til agrees with the Westminster Confession in stating that all creation is a revelation of the nature of God, and it is in this light that scriptures as redemptive revelation make sense. But if God can be known through general revelation and yet all knowledge is through the Bible, then there appears to be a discrepancy.

Like Kuyper, Van Til's view of the goal of the Christian life influences his approach to reason and knowing God. If humans, after regeneration, are restored to being able to use reason to understand God's revelation, then all the more it is incumbent upon believers to be able to show what is clear about God. This is not to say that such a demonstration is necessary to convert other; indeed, Paul maintains that clarity holds unbelievers inexcusable and is therefore a revelation of the justice of God. What kept Van Til from this fuller view of seeking and understanding?

Everyone Knows God

The answer is in Van Til's belief in the *sensus divinitatis* as the source of clarity and inexcusability which remained even after the Fall. Van Til's remedy for inexcusability was to claim that fallen men do in fact know God. It is not just that it is clear that God exists so that if men thought about it, if they cared to use reason, they could know. It is the case that this knowledge actually gets through to those in the fallen condition. That this was Van Til's view makes sense of his idea of the Fall as a particular violation of a command. Adam already knew God. The problem was in Adam's attitude, or heart. Not only are the invisible things of God displayed all around man, as well as in him, but they actually "get through."[29] Van Til gave as evidences of this fact the self-conscious activity of a person, a person's negative moral reaction to the revelation around him, a person's sense of dissatisfaction with all non-theistic interpretations, and the measure of involuntary recognition of the truth of the theistic interpretation as the true interpretation of the world. Van Til argued that these show that general revelation is known by all men.

Rather than solve the problem, this solution presents more problems. Van Til claimed that the knowledge of God is clear because men already know it. It is necessarily known. "The *intelligibility of anything, for man, presupposes the existence of God*—the God whose nature and character are delineated in God's revelation, found both in nature and in Scripture. It is this God—the only God—whom all men of necessity, 'know'."[30] According to Van Til, fallen humans "suppress" what they know in the sense of both knowing and trying not to know at the same time. This places the problem not as a problem of knowledge, but as a problem of desire. This creates a strange kind of person that both knows God as the source of all things good, and does not want what is good.[31] One is reminded of Satan as portrayed in Milton's *Paradise Lost*. In this work Satan rebels against God and God's view of the good and says, "Evil be thou my good."[32] Satan is still seeking what he thinks is good, he simply disagrees with the statement "God is good." It seems then that a person in this state actually has a difference of opinion over what is good, and hence they disagree ultimately with the claim that God is good. Does such a person know God? Certainly part of knowing God is knowing that God is good. Insofar as someone fails to know this of God, they are failing to know God. The sense in which all men know God is therefore left highly ambiguous. Van Til's view of clarity therefore seems to have some significant difficulties that spring from his view of inexcusability. For Van Til, humans are inexcusable for not acting on what they already know, rather than for failing to know what they should know (unbelief).

Furthermore, if all persons already know God, in what sense can it be said that they are sinning in not understanding? Do they both know and not understand? Greg Bahnsen produced his doctoral dissertation on the subject of self-deception in order to argue that all persons know God but deceive themselves about this knowledge. But the way that humans deceive themselves is by constructing an alternative that they claim to believe. If this alternative is inexcus-

able, it is inexcusable not because they also believe in God at the same time. All
this does is to point to an inconsistency, but not which side of the inconsistency
to reject. What must be demonstrated is that the alternative to belief in God,
which humans use to deceive themselves, is the result of not seeking and understanding what is clear. That is, it must be shown to be clearly false so that there
is no excuse for believing it. Thus, humans are involved in deceiving themselves
with an inexcusable worldview.

Guilt, Inexcusability and Clarity

The operative assumption throughout this work is that guilt assumes inexcusability. Humans are guilty for not having known what is clear about God. If
humans have known this even in their fallen state, then what is it that they are
guilty of? If it is that they have not given to God the worship due Him, then this
seems to follow from their not recognizing God as God (the Creator). This
seems to be a lack of knowledge that results in wrong action. Van Til affirmed
that general revelation is sufficient: "After the fall of man natural revelation is
still historically sufficient. It is sufficient for such as have in Adam brought the
curse of God upon nature. It is sufficient to render them without excuse."[33]
It is sufficient to hold humans inexcusable. But what exactly is enough for
that? The Apostle Paul seems to affirm that it is more than a bare knowledge of
God, rather it is a knowledge of God's eternal power and divine nature (much
more than a mere "higher power"). General revelation is enough to give that
knowledge. Van Til claimed that the Triune God is necessary for all knowledge.
For Van Til it is not that theism is one worldview among many that might have
some truths. It is that apart from theism no knowledge is possible at all. Wesley
A. Roberts said that according to Van Til, the most basic of all facts is the existence of the triune God.[34] The existence of the triune God is not simply reasonable or probably true, it is a necessary presupposition for any other belief. Consequently, Van Til held that unless a person believes in the triune God of the
Bible, no other belief could be logically supported.
In taking this position, Van Til affirmed logic. Either believe in God or lose
intelligibility. The assumption is that one would want a logical worldview. This
seems like a safe assumption, especially if logic is taken in the narrow sense as
the laws of inference. Again, here the law of non-contradiction shows up. Is it
that all non-Christian worldviews violate this law, while Christianity does not?
If so, then it seems that this law is necessary for knowledge. Or is it that only
theism provides us with the possibility of such a law, and therefore theism is
necessary for knowledge? Should reason be assumed in order to find the correct
worldview, or should theism be assumed in order to establish reason? The latter
appears to beg the question in that it assumes the law is desirable, and then uses
it to show that all non-Christian views violate it. The former is free from such
problems, and appears to be what the Hodges and Warfield were affirming. In
answering the question "how do I know" it is necessary to proceed from epistemology (reason) to ontology (the nature of being).

Presupposing Scripture

However, Van Til continued from this point to argue that it is the scriptures that are necessary for any knowledge. While Warfield argued that one must first have the scriptures proven as such, Van Til saw this as holding God to human standards of knowledge where God is the author of knowledge. It is certainly true that many people have rejected the scriptures for less than adequate "reasons." But this does not mean that the law of non-contradiction is an arbitrary standard invented by humans. Van Til believed that if anything is to be intelligible or coherent, it must be based on the truth of the Christian scriptures.[35] This is based on Van Til's view of Christ as the source of knowledge itself. The Apostle John speaks of Christ this way in John Chapter One. Van Til took the *logos* spoken of in John to refer to Christ and the scriptures, while others, like Gordon Clark[36] argued that *logos* should also be taken to refer to logic and hence the "word" is what illuminates men's minds even with respect to general revelation. Indeed, there seem to be five senses of the *logos* in John 1: The eternal Word of God (John 1:1–2); reason, the light of man (John 1:3–5); general revelation (John 1: 10); special revelation (John 1:11–13); and Jesus Christ (John 1:14). But for Van Til, the standard is the Bible itself.[37] It seems wrong to say that Warfield appealed to a non-Christian standard when speaking of "right reason" in that Warfield claimed right reason necessarily reveals God, and is therefore by no means a non-Christian standard.

However, it should be noted that Van Til did not argue that one must go to the scriptures for all kinds of knowledge. He explicitly said otherwise. He argued that there is nothing in the universe about which humans can have a full understanding unless the Bible is taken into account. This does not mean that a person should consult the Bible rather than the laboratory in order to understand the anatomy of a snake. But if a person only goes to the laboratory then he/she will not have a full understanding, or even a true interpretation, of the snake. According to Van Til, this reality makes it necessary for apologetics to have a definitely assigned place in the orthodox seminary.[38]

What Van Til said is that the knowledge of God derived from the scriptures is necessary for any other knowledge because it is the basic presupposition on which all else is founded. The question therefore remains: if the scriptures are necessary for a coherent world and life view, to what extent is general revelation enough to hold men inexcusable? If the scriptures are a redemptive revelation designed to explain how God will return humanity to the truth, then that truth must be available in the first place in order for a return to it to be a coherent notion. If general revelation reveals the eternal power and divine nature of God, then this is not a bare "higher power" but rather a full knowledge. Thus, general revelation is not simply a bare minimum.

Van Til and Warfield

Van Til viewed Warfield's system of apologetics as involving a stress on the objective, intelligible, and clear revelation of God to all humans.[39] This revelation is so objectively clear that it is not rational to reject the Christian faith. Van Til concurred with this part of Warfield's view. For Warfield, there was ideally only one science, and Christianity is the only intelligible system of truth. Van Til criticized Warfield however, because he saw Warfield's system as only providing "probability" rather than necessity. Van Til's principal argument was to show the absurdity of the contradiction. If the opposite is impossible then Christianity must be true (this is the use of the law of non-contradiction). In essence Van Til characterized Warfield as an evidentialist. There are aspects of Warfield's approach that can be characterized as evidentialist. Such an approach only establishes the probability of the Christian worldview and not the inexcusability of unbelief. Van Til maintained that Warfield argued for the probability of Christianity's truth. Van Til also argued that while there is only one science, those engaged in the scientific endeavor are subjectively and spiritually at war in their principles and goals. For Van Til the only way an unbeliever can contribute to the body of science is by departing from his principles and presuppositions. Van Til's emphasis was that on the natural man's principles nothing would be intelligible at all.[40]

It could be true that while Warfield provides the foundation for clarity and inexcusability, he did not develop this and remained content with probability. But does Van Til provide a framework for clarity and inexcusability? Just like Kuyper, Van Til held that the materialist worldview is the opposite of Christianity. Many of his arguments are directed against materialism. But if materialism is false, does this mean theism is true? Did not Plato also argue against materialism with his dualism? And spiritual monists also argue against materialism. While Van Til's method is sound (if the opposite is impossible Christianity is true), it is vitally important that this method find the real opposite—a contradiction rather than a contrary.

Van Til and Kuyper

Kuyper, on the other hand, avoided evidentialism with a view, as noted above, that can be called worldview relativism. Van Til saw Kuyper's main contribution as delineating that there are two basic principles at work, each of which produces a different worldview and hence two different "sciences." This was what Van Til saw as Kuyper's "distinctive and masterful insight into apologetics."[41] The two conflicting principles that are at work in the believer and unbeliever (God versus autonomy) result in two opposing theories of knowledge.[42] According to Van Til, the alienation from God due to sin has a significant impact on the natural man, in contrast to the enlightening work of the Holy Spirit in the regenerated man's mind.[43] Van Til agreed with Kuyper in maintaining that there is a different orientation in terms of attitude, or heart, that results in differ-ent lifestyles.[44] This is somewhat different than Warfield in that Warfield saw the difference with respect to the use of reason, not with respect to an attitude.

However, Van Til criticized Kuyper in his view of apologetics. Kuyper concluded that apologetics is essentially useless. Van Til saw this as a mistake in Kuyper, being inferred from the antithesis between belief and unbelief and the resulting two sciences.[45] For Kuyper there was little use for reasoning with the unbeliever since the unbeliever disagrees as to what makes a "reasonable" ar-gument. Van Til thought that Kuyper stumbled at this point in that God has clearly revealed Himself in nature and history so that the unbeliever is not doing justice to the objective facts when he does not submit to God as his Creator. And the unbeliever never ceases to be made in the image of God, and so it is only in thinking God's thoughts after him that a person can find an intelligible founda-tion for knowledge and experience.[46]

Van Til's Attempt to Preserve Inexcusability

Van Til affirmed that there is a clear revelation of God in nature and history and that the unbeliever must deny this in order to hold his fallen worldview. Thus, apologetics has the task of showing the unbeliever that his world and life view is incoherent. However, Van Til saw in Kuyper something that made him take Kuyper's position. He found it impossible to hold with Kuyper that because of the difference between the Christian and the non-Christian worldviews it is useless for the Christian to reason with the non-Christian. But he viewed War-field as asserting that the difference is only one of degree, which he also found unacceptable. And so he took the position of Kuyper without taking the position that reasoning between the Christian and the non-Christian is useless.[47] This seems to imply that there is a common basis for reasoning, or something that both the Christian and the non-Christian would accept as reason.

Greg Bahnsen argued that Van Til drew the best insights from Warfield and Kuyper and formed them into a transcendental, presuppositional apologetic that defeats all philosophical challenges to the biblical worldview.[48] Van Til did find something beneficial in both Warfield and Kuyper, and he stated this when he said that Warfield was correct in claiming that Christianity is objectively defen-sible, and that the natural man has the ability to understand. The natural man must be shown that on his own principles all truth and meaning is lost.[49] Van Til also argued, and this is part of the problem in his view of man mentioned above, that the unbeliever can understand Christianity intellectually while not under-standing it spiritually.[50]

Problems for Van Til

Even so, Van Til's analysis seems to leave some problems. Did Warfield really only allow for the probability of the truth of Christianity? Warfield said "without the knowledge of God it is not too much to say we know nothing rightly, so that the renunciation of the knowledge of God carries with it renunciation of all right knowledge."[51] That Warfield believed this seems contrary to how Van Til portrayed him. If Warfield followed Charles Hodge, and Hodge was arguing from the law of non-contradiction to the incoherence of all non-Christian views, does this really allow for the possibility that a non-Christian is true? If Warfield's position was that there is a right reason that is necessary for thought itself, and this reason reveals the eternal power and divine nature of God, then this seems to imply that reason leads only to belief in God. This establishes a foundation on which it can be argued that there is a clear general revelation of God's existence to all humans and that therefore unbelief is inexcusable and leaves humanity in need of redemption.

Similarly, Van Til's view of Kuyper presents some problems. If there are two worldviews, as Kuyper said, then it seems that both of them will claim that the other is incorrect (based on some standard that the other does not accept). Hence to say that the fallen worldview is incorrect because it is self-contradictory is simply to continue to affirm one's own presupposition. What is necessary is that there is rationality, which serves as a common ground for all humans, and reveals the existence of God. This is the method of apologetics, and, as Warfield said, there is only one science with a number of incorrect attempts at it. In this case, reason stands as the necessary precondition for thought. If the fallen worldview violates reason, then it is incoherent. This is certainly different from saying that only the theistic position allows for reason, which is what it seems Van Til tried to maintain.

Given the above considerations, Van Til's position uses circular reasoning. Van Til asked: "If it is true that the difference between Christian and anti-theistic epistemology is as fundamental as we have contended that it is, and if it is true that the antitheist takes his position for granted at the outset of his investigations, and if it is true that the Christian expects his opponent to do nothing else in as much as according to Scripture the 'natural man' cannot discern the things of the Spirit, we must ask *whether* it is then of any use for the Christian to reason with his opponent".[52] His answer was that the message must not be toned down by arguing that epistemological terminology means the same thing for theists and non-theists alike. There is almost always a difference when unbelievers use the term "reason" in contrast to when believers use the term "reason." Instead, the answer must be found in the concept of Christian theism, where God alone is absolute. It does not seem that Warfield would have disagreed with this conclusion. Certainly Warfield would have agreed that God only is absolute. That there is a "right reason" by which humanity comes to know God does not subordinate God to reason.

Worldviews and Circularity

In this sense all worldviews are circular in that all worldviews have assumptions. However, this does not mean that all assumptions are coherent. And it means that if an assumption/presupposition is incoherent, it is so because of some standard of thought that applies to all presuppositions. Van Til affirmed God as absolute, Darwin/Marx/Freud affirm matter as such, Plato the forms, etc. How can a person decide which presupposition to believe? If there is no method of deciding that is objective to all, then persons cannot be held accountable for making the "correct" decision. However, if there is such a method, then it is not the product of one of them but stands as judge over all. To argue that the Christian epistemology is the best, and that Christianity is necessary for this epistemology, is simply not an argument. Marx and Plato each say the same of their worldview. There appears to be a sense then in which reason, as the laws of thought, as what Reid was looking for, as the law of non-contradiction identified by Charles Hodge and Warfield, is transcendental. Reason is necessary for argumentation and hence cannot be argued against. While some people might try to argue against such laws, in their arguments they are assuming these laws and hence displaying their own inconsistency. Van Til's approach, showing the impossibility of the contradiction of Christianity, is a sound approach. However, it is reason that shows contradictions, not an affirmation of the existence of God. The latter is exactly what must be proven. If the proof is the transcendental proof argued for by Van Til (that God must be assumed to have any intelligibility at all), this seems to be coherent (provide meaning) only because the laws of identity, excluded middle, and non-contradiction are used to argue for the necessity of God. God is necessary for intelligibility because all other worldviews violate the law of non-contradiction and hence violate reason. In the most basic sense reason is necessary for intelligibility, and not all worldview presuppositions are coherent.

Conclusion

Van Til, as one of the prominent thinkers in Warfield's legacy, does contribute by expounding the notion of the Transcendental Argument and the necessity of realizing one's presuppositions. However, his explanation of inexcusability, clarity, and how God is known, has enough problems to make his apologetic approach suffer and become problematically circular. Inexcusability requires not circularity but the use of reason to establish one's presupposition. Reason, as the laws of thought, should not be confused with a presupposition because reason, as the laws of thought, is used for establishing any meaningful presupposition.

In concluding it is worth noting that Van Til, as a figure that was at both Princeton and Westminster Seminary, sought to provide an apologetic that would keep Westminster Seminary from going the way of Princeton. Was his Presuppositionalism sufficient for this task? Does it provide a foundation, not only for Westminster Seminary, but for Christianity? Or does it contain the same problems found in Hodge's view of faith, and Warfield's view of the blessing? And what foundation is necessary for a lasting institution of Christian education? Such questions require us to explore more contemporary attempts to provide an account of how God is known.

Questions:
1. What are presuppositions, and how can the presuppositions of a worldview be identified?
2. How does Van Til try to reconcile the differences between Warfield and Kuyper?
3. What is the Transcendental Argument?
4. How is Van Til's claim that scripture must be presupposed, an example of the use of reason? Which is more basic, scripture, or the use of reason?
5. Why does Van Til think that everyone knows God? Compare this with the claim that sin is a failure to seek, understand and do what is right.
6. How does Van Til's claim that humans know God but do not act on this knowledge fail to preserve inexcusability?
7. What is Bahnsen's view of self-deception? How do people deceive themselves, and how can this be used to show the need for reason and clarity?

CHAPTER 6:
ALVIN PLANTINGA AND WARRANTED
CHRISTIAN BELIEF

While liberal Christians tried to adopt Modernity and adapt Christianity, the demands of consistency led to a rejection of Christianity altogether. Princeton Theological was not able to maintain its original views about God and Christianity. As liberalism gave way to material monism of various sorts, Christian belief became suspect in the academy. Is a defense of the acceptability of Christian belief in the academy sufficient or even worth attempting? Or, in light of Christianity's claims about sin, must the foundation of the Christian worldview be established? And what is the role of intuition in knowing God? Is immediate and intuitive knowledge the highest expression of the knowledge of God or does Christianity call humans to something more?

While not part of the Princeton tradition, Alvin Plantinga has contributed to the discussion about reason and worldviews within the Reformed tradition. As one of the founders of the school of thought known as Reformed Epistemology, he has argued that Christian belief is warranted in contrast to the deeply ingrained belief found in the academy that Christian belief is intellectually deficient in some way. The properly basic beliefs on which the Christian worldview is founded are as warranted as other commonly held beliefs, such as the belief in other minds, the existence of the past, or the external world. He has developed this approach to be a response to criticisms of Christian belief from thinkers such as Freud, Marx, and Kant. But how does warrant fit in with the Christian claim that it is clear that God exists so that unbelief is inexcusable? Why do humans need redemption, and for what do I need to be forgiven? Does Plantinga's account of proper function make sense of the need for redemption, and preserve necessary concepts such as inexcusability, clarity, and rationality? In the following Plantinga's position will be described and then considered in light of the above questions. The assertion here is that Plantinga's position highlights the need for a natural theology that responds to challenges (defeaters); warrant is lost when defeaters are raised, and thus in order to preserve warrant these defeaters must be addressed. If there is no excuse for unbelief, then there can be no unanswerable defeaters. While Plantinga has established that Christians are within their epistemic rights,[1] there is still the further work of showing that the Christian claim that there is no excuse for unbelief is coherent. Can defeaters be successfully responded to, specifically defeaters about the existence and knowledge of God? In this chapter I will argue that while Plantinga does good work in responding to one level of criticism against Christian belief, much more is needed to successfully respond to that challenge.

Plantinga and Warranted Christian Belief

Plantinga's project is to respond to the *de jure* objection to Christian belief. This objection says that Christian belief is somehow intellectually sub par. It is exemplified in thinkers like Freud and Marx. Plantinga defines Christian belief as the belief embodied in the Apostle's Creed and Nicene Creed, or the intersection of beliefs in more recent works like the New Catholic Catechism, the Heidelberg Catechism, the Augsburg Confession and the Westminster Catechism.[2] He believes that these affirm: God created the heavens and earth; he created human beings in his own image; human beings fell ruinously into sin which requires salvation; God sent Christ, who is the eternal Son of God and became incarnate, suffered and died as the atonement for sin, rose from the dead and thus enabled humans to be redeemed to have eternal life.[3] "These beliefs are ordinarily thought of as paradigmatically Christian and ordinarily referred to by the term 'Christian.'"[4] It is his project to inquire into the epistemological status of these beliefs, and his conclusion is that they are warranted (as opposed to intellectually sub par, but also in contrast to being in need of justification as required by Enlightenment thinkers).

The initial warrant of Christian belief is based on the *sensus divinitatis*. He calls this the Aquinas and Calvin model, and describes it in the following way: Humans were created in the image of God, with an intellect, affects and will (the broad image of God) all of which were originally in close contact with, and extensive knowledge of, God (the narrower image of God) "They loved and hated what was lovable and hateful; above all, they knew and loved God."[5] The Fall had implications for the image of God in man. "In particular, the *sensus divinitatis* has been damaged and deformed; because of the Fall, we no longer know God in the same natural and unproblematic way in which we know each other and the world around us."[6] Indeed, humans now resist the *sensus divinitatis*, and we fight against it and this lands us in a quagmire. We are unable to get ourselves out of this, and it requires the grace of God, through the atonement of Christ and the renewing work of the Holy Spirit, to redeem humans.

Plantinga refers to C.S. Lewis and his book *Mere Christianity* as support for his description of Christian belief. But he also made mention of the historic development of Christianity, from the Apostles' Creed to Westminster. How does mere Christianity, this version given by Plantinga, compare to the work of the creeds? In this version of Christianity, what we might call a soteriological version (it focuses on salvation), what is the original work given to humanity before the Fall, and what is the relationship of a redeemed human to that original work? Understanding Plantinga's relationship to historic Christianity, and his vision of the goal of the Christian life, will help us better understand how there is benefit to be found in his work, but also places to go further. Could his defense of Christian belief serve as a foundation to protect Christianity against the challenges that moved Harvard and Princeton?

Plantinga and the de jure Objection

The *de jure* question deals with whether or not it is rational, reasonable, justifiable, or warranted to believe in Christianity, or if Christian beliefs is somehow intellectually defective.[7] Plantinga considers a number of such objections, a notable example of which is W.K. Clifford. Clifford maintained, in his "The Ethics of Belief," that it is unjustifiable to believe anything without evidence. Plantinga disagrees, citing William James's essay "The Will to Believe," and using examples where forced and live option, without any contrary evidence, require belief. But he also examines Locke, who, living at the end of a period of history cluttered with religious wars, sought rational means to secure unity. In arguing against basing belief in religious affections, Locke encouraged the use of reason to guide belief formation. In this view, a person is justified in accepting a belief only if it is either properly basic, self-evident, incorrigible, or evident to the senses.[8] But Plantinga points out that this would mean that almost none of our beliefs are justified, and these requirements do not withstand their own standard if applied to themselves.

Indeed, either this standard is wrong, or most of our beliefs are unjustified including Plantinga's belief that there is a snow in the backyard and that he held class yesterday. These are beliefs that he holds in the basic way, but that do not conform to the standards proposed by Locke. In terms of these kinds of basic beliefs, Plantinga says, "Of course I realize I could be mistaken; but am I flouting duty in so believing? I reflect on the matter as carefully as I can; I simply see no duty here—and not because I doubt the existence of duties generally, or of epistemic duties specifically.[9] Plantinga then asks, "Can I be blameworthy for believing in this way?"

Next, he considers a "standard" Christian believer. She doesn't believe in Christianity based on propositional evidence, so she believes in the basic way. She has read objections to Christianity from Freud, Marx, and Nietzsche (among others), but doesn't think they are correct. She also knows of the theistic arguments, but doesn't base her spirituality on them. Instead she looks to the kind of life exemplified in Jonathan Edwards's *Religious Affections*. "Is she then going contrary to duty in believing as she does? Is she being irrational? Clearly not. There could be something *defective* about her, some malfunction not apparent on the surface. She could be *mistaken*, a victim of illusion or wishful thinking, despite her best efforts."[10] Nonetheless, she is not violating any epistemic duty, she is doing her best and she is justified, and this is not only true, but obviously true (according to Plantinga).

Defeaters

Warrant can be lost when defeaters are raised. "Defeaters are reasons for giving up a belief *b* you hold."[11] Plantinga considers different kinds of defeaters, like rebutting defeaters, undercutting defeaters, rationality defeaters and warrant defeaters. In Plantinga's examples these all have to do with beliefs based on sense perception (a sheep in the field, red widgets in the factory, a barn along the road) and the faculties used to arrive at these beliefs (or the conditions that affected the senses). Thus, when a challenge is raised about the environment in which your senses operated (say, a special light that made things appear red that are not ordinarily red), then this is a defeater. Or, many fake barns among real barns, so that your claim about a magnificent barn may actually be about a fake barn.

Defeaters have temporal and personal qualifications. What counts as a defeater at one time might not have been a defeater at an earlier time, or for one person but not another.[12] The kind of defeater that *de jure* challenges raise is that Christian belief is not formed by a truth-aimed process. Or, as Freud says, while it is formed by a properly functioning faculty, it is based on wish fulfillment and this is not aimed at truth. Plantinga responds to Freud's criticism with skill, and his work on this is an example of why natural theology is necessary. Indeed, Plantinga can be said to "deconstruct" Freud and Marx, by taking apart their complaint and analyzing it for rational consistency. He notes that they do not prove that Christian belief is sub par, but simply announce it.[13] This announcement simply presupposes that theistic belief is false without proving as much. Plantinga's work highlights the need for natural theology precisely because what he is doing is taking away any excuse that Freud and Marx have; they might come up with reasons to think that theism is false. Can these be responded to or can they be used as an excuse for rejecting theism?

Beyond Freud's criticism, the two main defeaters that Plantinga considers (and offers defeaters against) are the problem of evil and the reality of religious pluralism. In doing this he outlines what is necessary to defeat a defeater. A response must contain not simply premises that an advanced academic would understand, but be such that when a person sees the defeater he/she is required to give up the conclusion.[14] An argument is one way to defeat a defeater, but Plantinga thinks there is a better way. That is, put me in a position to have an experience, such that with that experience the rational thing to do is give up the defeater.

The Loss and Return of Warrant through Religious Experience

Warrant can be lost, but it can also be regained. Plantinga's explanation of this relies on experience. The initial loss of close, intimate knowledge of God was due to the Fall which distorted the *sensus divinitatis* and had repercussions throughout human nature. It is restored by the Holy Spirit in the work of regeneration. After regeneration, persons are once again able to have intuitive knowledge of God. This is like the other senses humans have in that it is not inferred but is immediate. Although it is dependent on the work of the Holy Spirit, one can put oneself in position to have such experiences. Encouraging people to do this, as opposed to giving argument from natural theology, is much more helpful in the process of encouraging them to know God. After all, people don't convert through a cold reasoning process, but instead conversion is more along the lines of what Jonathan Edwards inspired in the First Great Awakening. The "ordinary" Christian continues to be warranted, even after having read Freud and Marx, because his/her Christian beliefs are formed in a basic way, and the criticisms of Fred and Marx do not negate the immediate reality of the *sensus divinitatis*.

It is because of this line of thinking that Plantinga does not see much need for a fully developed natural theology. But how helpful is an appeal to religious experience? Plantinga considers religious pluralism and argues that the fact of various religious experiences in the world does not count as a defeater to Christian belief. But what about the same belief interpreted in different ways? The defeater is not that Christian belief is false because of other religions, but that the Christian interpretation of the *sensus divinitatis* is a misinterpretation.

Plantinga's examples about beliefs formed in a basic way all involved sense perception or authority. I see a sheep on a hill, I see red widgets in the factory, I see a barn by the road, I believe that the University of Aberdeen was founded in a certain year because their current catalog says it was. Defeaters to these call into question the environment in which my senses operate, or the reliability of an authority. But what about when we make the move from simply reporting what I sense, to explaining what it is (i.e. giving an interpretation)? Here is where we get into the work of philosophy—living the examined life. A person may remain warranted in believing in God after reading Nietzsche because they formed their belief in God in a basic way and Nietzsche offers no objection that calls this into question. But what about when a person notices that many others who had a similar sense arrived at very different conclusions about that sense? Or, without being aware of anyone else, what about when the person realizes that his/her intuitions have often been mistaken, and wants more than simply warrant? I might be warranted, but is this sufficient to be without excuse?

Plantinga, the Westminster Catechism, and the Goal of the Christian Life

Plantinga's description of the original state of mankind was that humans had an immediate, intuitive knowledge of God that resulted in a close and loving relationship. Thus, his view of redemption is that humans are restored to this, and their final state is having this in perfection. He finds support for this in the Westminster Catechism. As noted earlier, the first question to the Shorter Catechism asks, "What is the chief end of man?" The answer is that "the chief end of man is to glorify God and enjoy him forever." Plantinga understands this as perceiving, noting, appreciating, delighting in, and relishing God's glory.[15] He quotes Jonathan Edwards as describing the joy he will have in being wrapped up in God in heaven, and C.S. Lewis who describes a child making mud-pies who is unable to understand how much better a vacation at sea will be.[16]

We've already seen how a similar understanding was found in Warfield and Augustine. The two problems discussed are that this knowledge is primarily immediate instead of through the work of understanding and drawing inferences, and second that it is postponed to the future state of heaven rather than seen as necessary now. But in order to better understand Plantinga we can also focus on how he understands the Fall. What was the Fall that brought corruption to human nature and the loss of the *sensus divinitatis*?

In the Fall, Adam and Eve are approached by a tempter who offers defeaters. He raises questions about their belief-forming process: "Did God really say, 'You must not eat from any tree in the garden'?" (Genesis 3:1). Eve repeats the command, but gets it slightly wrong. Then the tempter follows up with an alternative interpretation: "You will not surely die . . . For God knows that when you eat of it your eyes will be opened, and you will be like God, knowing good and evil" (3:4). Eve sees that the fruit is pleasing to the eye, and believes the tempter's interpretation that it is desirable for gaining wisdom, and so she eats, gives it to Adam, and he eats.

Here we have elements that are directly relevant to Plantinga's view of basic beliefs, warrant, and defeaters. According to Plantinga, Adam and Eve started off with beliefs about God formed in a basic (intuitive) way. They perceived God directly and had a relationship with him. Further, God gives them commands that they are to follow. But when tested, this kind of knowledge was not sufficient to prevent them from falling away. Indeed, it was revealed that they did not have a very good understanding of the commands of God (Eve gets the command wrong), which raises questions about how close their relationship was after all (if they were so close, why didn't they pay better attention?). If this close intuitive relationship, and the *sensus divinitatis*, is not enough to get people to pay attention to the commands of God, then what is? The temptation reveals that their relationship with God was not all that it should have been.

This is directly relevant to how Plantinga proposes a modern Christian can be warranted. Granting that Eve had this intuitive knowledge of God and was therefore warranted in her belief in God—as is the person in the examples given by Plantinga and discussed earlier (page 100 of *Warranted*)—what the tempter did was raise a question about how she interpreted this intuition. The command of God is only as reliable as the one who gave it, and the tempter offers an alternative interpretation about the one who gave it (God). What Eve needs is not a stronger conviction about her intuition (this would also be an intuition that would be open to the same kind of questioning about interpretation). What Eve needs is a way to reject alternative interpretations.

She could have had such a response if she had been developing a knowledge of God that went further than the intuitive, that did the work of drawing inferences from her belief in God. What the tempter suggests is that God's concern is that if Adam and Eve eat the fruit they will know good and evil the way that God knows good and evil. The crux of the alternative interpretation is that humans can know good and evil the way that God knows good and evil. But Eve could have drawn out inferences about God: God as creator determines what is good and evil by creating the nature of things; humans cannot know in this way, but only know good and evil by discovering and learning about the nature of things. Therefore, this alternative interpretation is based on impossibility: Temporal, finite humans can be like the eternal, infinite God. On this basis the alternative can be rejected.

This has a bearing on how Plantinga understands the goal of the Christian life. Regeneration restores the *sensus divinitatis*, and the blessing is had in heaven where humans have an intuitive, immediate, close relationship with God. Building on the problems with this discussed earlier (Warfield and Augustine), how does this fit in with what was needed to overcome the temptation? Beyond the immediate, intuitive knowledge of God, do humans also need to be able to draw inferences to increase their knowledge of God (not simply to overcome temptation)? The temptation revealed that Adam and Eve did not have a close relationship with God, they did not understand the most basic thing about God: God alone is the creator, and nothing in the creation—humans included—can have knowledge the way God has knowledge. Wouldn't a closer relationship with God be one where humans not only had the *sensus divinitatis*, but also drew out all the good and necessary inferences that lead to greater understanding of God? To say that these could be given immediately and directly as well is to say that they would be susceptible to the temptation—a further intuition is not sufficient to respond to the temptation because the temptation is about how to interpret intuitions. In order to respond to the temptation what is needed is inferential knowledge.

Thus, if we are going to agree with the Westminster Catechism, then glorifying God and enjoying him forever requires knowing God through inferential knowledge; indeed, such knowledge is a "higher" knowledge than is the *sensus divinitatis* because it is able to withstand tests such as the temptation. Furthermore, this is not merely in response to defeaters from critics. Inferential knowledge of God is not necessary simply because the tempter came along—this is backwards. The tempter was testing to see if Adam and Eve knew God as they should have before he came along. This test revealed that they didn't have a close relationship with God. They did not know the basic things about God. To maintain that the goal of redemption is simply a return to the original state is to by-pass the work of knowing God that was given to man in the beginning. Knowing God requires work in that it requires inferred knowledge about God from the creation and works of God. Thus, the need for redemption does not override this work of knowing God, but adds an additional aspect to knowing God; not only do the works of creation and providence reveal the nature of God, but so does the work of redemption.

The Knowledge of God

Plantinga discusses the Christian who has read the critics, is not impressed, and stays within his/her epistemic rights of Christian belief based on the *sensus divinitatis*. But is this person doing the work of inferring even more knowledge of God so that not only is his/her impression of the critics "not impressed," but he/she is able to show why the critics are without excuse? What happens when an alternative interpretation of this person's *sensus divinitatis* is given? Does the person simply shrug his/her shoulders and say "I believe what I believe"? Is this really the response that best illustrates a close relationship to God? Or does a close relationship entail the ability to respond to the tempter not only by vindicating one's knowledge of God, but showing why the tempter's interpretation is impossible and without excuse? A close relationship requires the latter. And while Plantinga does admirable work in confronting Freud and Marx with their inconsistencies, he also defends the attitude that simply falls back on the *sensus divinitatis*. Is this the maturity and fullness of Christian belief, the highest expression to be found in heaven, or is it the starting point that requires further growth? The temptation and Fall reveal that simple reliance on intuitive knowledge is insufficient. Plantinga may be correct that humans are fallen and in need of redemption to restore the *sensus divinitatis*, but that is only the beginning. Once redeemed, humans need to do the work of inferential knowledge in order to know God better, and in order to reply to temptation.

Part of why Plantinga defends the ordinary believer's warrant is that he points out, correctly, that very few people, perhaps no one, converts through a theistic proof, and memorizing a proof seems dry and lifeless compared to the spiritual life exemplified by Jonathan Edwards. Kelly James Clark advocates a similar approach to knowing God, and three approaches to proof God's existence.[17] The first is the evidentialist approach, which agrees with the Enlightenment that a belief should only be held upon adequate evidence. This view says that there is adequate evidence for belief in God. The second also agrees with the enlightenment, but believes that there is not adequate evidence for belief in God. The problem with these first two approaches is what has been outlined by Plantinga and noted above, in addition to their inability to inspire spiritual devotion.

The third view rejects the enlightenment claim, and argues instead that there are certain beliefs people hold without evidence, and that they are rational in doing so. This last view Clark identifies with Plantinga. The example Clark gives is of his grandmother, who is a sincere believer in God, but cannot prove God exists. However, every religion is filled with sincere grandmothers with grandsons wanting to defend them. And yet, according to Christianity, these grandmothers have sinned in failing to seek and understand and are therefore inexcusable. Why should Clark think his grandmother is any different? Do grandmothers, Christian or not, need to seek and understand? Is the failure to do so a sin? Or do they get a pass on this and are therefore not required to live the examined life? A simple believer who relies on the *sensus divinitatis* and believes that he/she has a close relationship with God is in the same place as Eve just before the temptation. But what if this person is never tempted in that way, and is left alone to feel that they have a close relationship but in reality this relationship could be easily shown to be based on an inadequate understanding?

What the above shows is not that Plantinga is wrong about the warrant of Christian belief, but that his view requires expansion and development which in turn requires that Christians develop their basic beliefs, through inference, into a fuller knowledge of God. It is this latter that can respond to the tempter in a satisfactory manner. It is this that can not only show Freud and Marx that they are wrong about Christian belief, but that their own beliefs are without excuse. This requires getting into the worldview of Freud or Marx and doing the work of showing the points where they made mistakes, and where they thought that they were justified but were not. This is to go further than the requirements of W.K. Clifford (do not believe without proof); it is to say that even if there are some basic beliefs that do not require proof, one has an obligation to make inference and be able to respond to alternatives (i.ei. lead the examined life). Furthermore, if Christianity is true and unbelief is without excuse, then the redeemed Christian should be able to demonstrate that unbelief is without excuse.

Christian Obligation

But does the Christian have this obligation? Plantinga has often asserted that he does not, that belief in God is properly basic and therefore needs no argument or proof. However, because Christianity includes the claim that humans ought to know that God exists, adherence to Christianity requires more than intuition, or tradition and custom. For Christianity's claim to be true, the existence of God must be clear to all humans, so that a person must reject what is clear in order to avoid believing in God. Plantinga presents Christianity as one worldview among many, and argues that the adherents of Christianity are warranted in their Christian belief. Part of Christian belief is that humans are guilty for not knowing God as they should and that therefore they need redemption. Humans should believe in Christ for their redemption. However, Plantinga does not show why non-Christians should be Christians. Terrence Tilley says "He [Plantinga] has not shown why his position is not arbitrary or making the mistake of presuming what is at issue."[18] If humans are inexcusable for failing to know God, then it must be clear that God exists. If it is clear that God exists then human rationality is necessary to know this. Therefore, claims about proper/improper function cannot over-ride human rationality and the ability to know God. The Christian should be able to show that God exists, in order to show that humans are without excuse in their unbelief.

This problem may be connected to mistaking basic beliefs for intuitive/immediate beliefs. The latter can be distinguished from logically basic beliefs. A logically basic belief is one that is presupposed by other beliefs, and the most basic belief would be that belief which is presupposed by all other beliefs. Thus, while an intuition is immediate and no act of inference was used to arrive at its conclusion, this must be distinguished from the act of interpreting the intuition. What is God, who is the source of the *sensus divinitatis*? Could you be like God, knowing good and evil the way God does? The intuition of God is not able to respond without the work of inferences. Further intuition will only encounter the same problem. Inferences are necessary for a full knowledge of God.

By noting that the interpretation I give to my intuitively basic beliefs has assumptions, I am examining my life and getting to a better understanding of how I think about the world. This gets me to logically basic beliefs. Eve's beliefs about God are more basic than her beliefs about how she can know good and evil. The tempter was calling her assumptions into question. An intuition is unhelpful at this point; what Eve must do is consider her logically basic beliefs. If God is the creator, then Eve cannot know good and evil the way God does. But is God the creator? This is precisely what the tempter is asking. To respond by saying that one has a *sensus divinitatis* does not help—the tempter will reply "but why rely on that?" Indeed, in Genesis 3 Eve continues to rely on sense data rather than drawing inferences—she makes her choice based on the fact that the fruit is pleasing to the eye and that she has no response to the tempter's claim that it is good for attaining wisdom.

What Plantinga's work highlights is the need to identify the logically basic beliefs of Christianity, and do the work of testing them. Is it true that God is the creator, or is the material universe eternal (without beginning)? Or perhaps God and the universe are co-eternal. Or perhaps there is no material universe, only pure consciousness. World history is full of such alternative interpretations that call the simple interpretation of the *sensus divinitatis* into question. A response is not necessary merely to feel satisfied that the critics have been answered; a response is necessary in order to know God better. As long as Plantinga views the goal of the Christian life to be the direct, intuitive, knowledge of God, he will not place value on the work required to draw out inferences about the creation and providence of God in order to grow in understanding.

Conversion and Reason

But what about the claim that no one ever converted based on a theistic argument, and that the spiritual life of a Jonathan Edwards is more attractive that the dry life of reason? There is enough truth here that these could be tempting. According to Christianity, people convert after the regenerating work of the Holy Spirit and in response to the preaching of the Gospel, not in response to theistic proofs. Granted. And if a person claims to have reasons, but shows very little concern or emotional engagement with life, this raises questions about how moving such proofs are. This leads some to give the interpretation that reason and proofs are secondary or not important, but there is an alternative interpretation.

What is taking place when persons converts is that they are being offered an interpretation of their life and are accepting it, in contrast to their previous understanding. This new interpretation can vary in sophistication and maturity. It can simply be: "You are a sinner and have made a mess of your life; only Christ can repair this." But such an account often requires great amounts of common ground between the presenter and the audience. Given to a person from a completely different cultural background these terms (sinner, Christ, repair) would need explanation. Thus, what is happening, even in these "simple" cases, is that a person is being asked to make inferences based on their intuitions, not simply to cling to intuitions. "This makes sense of your life; your previous beliefs do not." The person responds with: "Yes, it makes sense of *A*, *B*, and *C*, it gives meaning to these." The concern is one of meaning, and meaning requires inferences, not simply the *sensus divinitatis*.

The person who claims to have used reason and understands the proofs, but does not seem very "emotionally engaged" can be explained in a number of ways, including personality characteristics. But the real concern here is probably the claim that the intellect is insufficient and what is needed is "heart knowledge." This comes into direct conflict with the claims of scripture in that Jesus says it is the truth that sets a person free (John 8:32), and with philosophy which places emphasis on the need to lead the examined life in order to change one's life for the better. But it is also presuming that the person who claims to understand but yet still acts contrary to this really does have understanding. It is as if Eve, after eating the fruit, were to say, "I know God; my problem is self-control." Many might be tempted to agree with her and say, "yeah, she had the *sensus divinitatis* so she knew God." However, how can it be maintained that such a person knows God when the support they give for eating the fruit is that they can know good and evil the way God does? This is a failure to know God. A person who says "I know but I can't get my will into conformity with my mind" needs to be called on this claim. Do you know, or do you only think you know? Indeed, your actions reveal that you only think you know, but your knowledge is lacking and so you act in this way. Again, this is a call for further inferential knowledge, not a stronger assertion of the *sensus divinitatis*.

Plantinga's Use of Scripture and the Holy Spirit

In order to give some support to his worldview Plantinga sometimes makes an appeal to scripture, or the work of the Holy Spirit. However, appeals to scripture become circular, and the operations of the Holy Spirit are not what humans are accountable for. While a person may gain knowledge of the Gospel from scripture, why is the Gospel necessary? Why do humans need to be forgiven by

God? According to the Apostle Paul, the sin for which all humans are guilty is the failure to know God, which is due to not seeking and understanding and leads to not doing what is right. The need to believe in Christ for forgiveness arises precisely because one needs to be forgiven, forgiven for not knowing God as one should and could have. The scriptures are the account of God's redemption. This means that the scriptures are necessary because humans have first failed to know God as they should. The scriptures are not the source of this knowledge of God. Scripture claims that the heavens declare the glory of God (Psalm 19), and humans are responsible before God to know this. Therefore, appeals to the scripture as proof for the existence of God, or defending belief in God, beg the question.

Plantinga makes a similar appeal to the Holy Spirit. While it is true that the Reformed faith believes that the Holy Spirit is responsible for giving life to a person lost in the death of unbelief, this does not tell us about human responsibility. Plantinga's view of free will (libertarianism) and his solution to the problem of evil (Molinism) are explicitly rejected by Calvin (see his commentary on Romans) and the Westminster Confession of Faith (God brings all things to pass for the revelation of his glory and not for anything seen in the creature). For Plantinga to appeal to the Holy Spirit, and claim his understanding of the operations of the Holy Spirit is the Reformed view, is misleading. Warfield, as noted earlier, had a different understanding of the operations of the Holy Spirit and based his understanding on scripture and the Confession. Humans are responsible before God to know what is clearly revealed about God in the creation. Humans are not responsible for the work of the Holy Spirit. Therefore, appeals to the Holy Spirit as proof do nothing to establish human responsibility before God (to say nothing of the fact that such appeals are implemented by competing worldviews). Whether or not the Holy Spirit works in a person's life, that person is responsible to know what is clear about God.

In this history of Christianity it has been affirmed that after the Fall humans are not able to know God as they should. Augustine developed this more than others before him, and the Westminster Confession of Faith affirms this view. Sometimes this is expressed in saying that humans no longer have free will. This is true when understood to mean that after the Fall humans cannot do otherwise than sin. But how does this relate to responsibility? If humans cannot do otherwise how are they responsible? The Christian tradition has not merely rested in saying they are responsible due to imputed guilt, but has developed how this works out for the individual. Augustine, Luther and Calvin all distinguished between ability and liberty. Although ability may change, liberty does not, because while *ought* implies *can*, *can* implies *want*. For me to complain about this consequence by saying I am not responsible would be to say one of two things: I want to be able to not seek and not understand and yet not suffer the necessary consequence (which is logically impossible and therefore an incoherent complaint), or, I want to seek and understand in order to avoid the consequences of a darkened mind. Only this second complaint makes sense, and the reply is: Go ahead and start seeking. It makes no sense to say that one wants to seek, but cannot because all that is required to seek is the desire to do so.

Plantinga does rely on Romans 1:20 to support his view. He says "According to St. Paul, it is *unbelief* that is a result of dysfunction, brokenness, failure to function properly, or impedance of rational faculties. Unbelief, he says, is a result of sin; it originates in an effort, as Romans 1 puts it, to 'suppress the truth in unrighteousness.'"[19] There are two problems with his understanding of Romans 1. First, he takes it as self-evident, whereas the non-believer will ask for proof that it is clear that God exists (why believe Paul?). If the Christian has been renewed, healed, made to properly function, etc., then the Christian should be able to show that it is clear that God exists. Second, Plantinga skips over how clarity is suppressed. It is suppressed in unrighteousness, not in improper function (the former being a moral action, whereas improper function is simply how I find myself, as he notes in the footnote about John 9:2). It could be suggested that God immediately reveals himself to everyone at some point, and this is what makes them inexcusable. But how does this make sense of possible alternative interpretation of such an intuition? Inexcusability requires not only an intuition, but that alternative interpretations of that intuition are incoherent.

Conclusion

In the above we have seen much that can be of benefit in Reformed Epistemology and Plantinga. Indeed, the work Plantinga does in rejecting the claims of Freud and Marx exemplifies what can be done in natural theology. However, Plantinga's view of the blessed life in heaven gets in the way and prevents him from developing implications in his beliefs about the Fall and the need for redemption. The temptation revealed that Adam and Eve did not know God as they should have, and intuitive knowledge was not sufficient because what is being questioned is how to interpret the intuition. The Christian claim that humans need redemption from sin through the death of Christ makes sense only if that for which humans need redemption is a clear standard knowable to all human beings so that they are without excuse. Inexcusability requires clarity, and clarity requires inferential knowledge. This involves showing that the denial of belief in God is not rational, and that alternative interpretations are not coherent. Thus, the Christian, if restored to proper function, should be able to show that it is clear that God exists so that alternative interpretations are inexcusable.

Questions:
1. What does Plantinga mean by "warrant" and "proper function"?
2. What, according to Plantinga, is the cause of unbelief?
3. Why is Plantinga's account of sin and improper function insufficient to preserve the Christian claim that unbelief is inexcusable?
4. Why does the need to prove that God exists make the initial warrant of theistic belief of little value?

5. How might Warfield respond to Plantinga's view of the role of the Holy Spirit in renewing the *sensus divinitatis*?
6. What is the difference between an immediate belief and a logically basic belief?
7. What is required to live the examined life?
8. Plantinga relies on appeals to the Fall and then to the regenerating work of the Holy Spirit in restoring the *sensus divinitatis*. How might this be used to show the need for inferential knowledge of God?
9. What is Plantinga's view of heaven and his interpretation of the Westminster Catechism? How might this be understood differently?
10. Explain what happens in conversion, and how this is an inferential act in the search for meaning.
11. Explain what is happening when a person claims to know but not act accordingly. How does this relate to Eve and the temptation?
12. If humans in the fallen condition are not free to do otherwise, then how can they be responsible for not seeking and not understanding?

CHAPTER 7:
ON THE NECESSITY FOR NATURAL THEOLOGY
(Written with Surrendra Gangadean)

The challenges of Modernity continued to build throughout the 20th century. In light of these, can Christianity continue as a meaningful worldview apart from establishing the basis for its claim that humans have failed to seek and understand? Are the beliefs that Christianity claims humans have failed to understand meaningful, or even capable of being understood?

The tendency after Warfield and the change at Princeton which encouraged Van Til and others to leave and start Westminster Theological Seminary has been away from natural theology (NT). Whether in the form of Van Til's Presuppositionalism which claims that all people deep down know that God exists, so that the problem is in the will not the intellect, or Plantinga's Warranted Christian Belief in which NT is downplayed in favor of the *sensus divinitatis*, NT as the study of general revelation has been largely ignored. If Christianity maintains that unbelief is inexcusable, can it show this? What about those that honestly report not believing in God (vs. Van Til) and do not have the *sensus divinitatis*? Can the worldviews they do hold be shown to be founded on false basic beliefs? This work falls into the area of NT, and presupposes that there is a clear general revelation. The alternative undermines the redemptive claims of Christianity, and makes knowledge impossible (nothing is clear).

Natural theology attempts to show what can be known of God and man and good and evil from general revelation. Skepticism in general maintains knowledge is not possible hence natural theology is not possible. Fideism in general maintains that proof for one's first principles is not necessary hence natural theology is not necessary. Before engaging in its program NT must show why proof is necessary and how knowledge is possible. The possibility, necessity, and extent of the knowledge of God become more evident in historic Christian theism which is based on the over-arching and under-girding themes of Creation, Fall, and Redemption. The necessity of natural theology to know the glory of God is affirmed in the Westminster Confession of Faith (1.1, 2.2, 3.3, 4.1, 5.1, 6.1). Furthermore, this knowledge comes through the study of the works of God, and not through a direct, immediate vision of God in the afterlife.

A person's understanding of the necessity for natural theology will be in relation to that person's view of the goal of the Christian life. If the goal is justification (salvation), and this is communicated in special revelation, then there is little or no need for natural theology. If justification, occurring after regeneration, is a return to seeking, understanding, and doing what is right, then it is a return to the work of natural theology that was given to humanity in the beginning before the Fall and the need for special revelation. Indeed, the sin that humanity needs redemption from is the sin of not seeking and not understanding, which leads to emptiness and the manifestation of this in various forms of unrighteousness. The restoration is not merely to setting aside unrighteousness but to finding "the good" in seeking and understanding God (as opposed to determining good and evil for one's self). The believer not only says "I no longer want to be unrighteous," but "I want to find joy in understanding God so that I no longer fill my life in other ways." This makes natural theology necessary and supremely important. It is not simply a tool of apologetics; it is the source of joy in a believer's life.

It is often asserted that arguments do not make Christians. The best natural theology can fail to convert. This is a mistaken focus. Conviction of sin and death, and the need for redemption in Christ, leads to conversion. But what is sin and death? What is the sinner being redeemed from and restored to? If sin is the failure to seek, understand, and do what is right and death is the resulting emptiness and burning in unfulfilled desires that leads to unrighteousness, then restoration is seeking and understanding. To try and avoid unrighteousness apart from finding joy in seeking to know God in all that by which he makes himself known will not be successful. Natural theology is therefore necessary not as a means to convert others but as a source of joy in the life of every believer. Do believers find joy in seeking and understanding God? What is the result of not finding one's joy in this way?

Skepticism

In the history of skepticism, from ancient to contemporary, the basis of skepticism has shifted. At times it is grounded metaphysically in various formulations of the problem of the one and the many. At other times it is grounded epistemologically in variations of empiricism and rationalism. Most recently it has been grounded in hermeneutics, in issues related to interpreting experience and constructing worldviews. From time to time it has been grounded in the nature of knowledge itself, whether knowledge is discursive, cognitive, and propositional, or whether it is relational, mystical, and a matter of encounter.

Metaphysical skepticism denies there is an object of knowledge. In the ancient world this was done in two ways: either all is flux (becoming without being—Heraclitus, or all is dukkha, dependently co-arising—Buddhism), or all is permanent (being without becoming—Parmenides, or all is one, beyond all dualities—Shankara's Advaita). Where all is permanent, change is an illusion (maya). Where all is change, permanence is an illusion (no object, no self). Since knowledge of the world involves permanence and change (some change in permanence and some permanence in change), on the assumption that all is one (either change or permanence), knowledge is not possible. The dualism of Plato and Aristotle attempted to address the problem of permanence and change but left significant problems unresolved.

Epistemological skepticism reckons with the limits of experience and reason as they have been used in the modern period (Enlightenment). Experience may come through ordinary sense experience (common sense), or sense experience systematically pursued (science), or through inner experience (intuition). Ordinary experience gives appearance and not reality (Is the ocean blue? Does the sun rise?). Furthermore, through sense experience we cannot know there is an external world or material substance (Berkeley), nor causality or a self as perceiver (Hume). Science does not attempt to show that the external world exists, or that all is matter, or that matter is eternal. Naturalism is the methodological assumption of science and empiricism, held on pragmatic grounds, with a tentativeness which disinvites philosophical criticism. Intuition admits of no corrective process. But neither are the deliverances of intuition self-certifying. Truth (or goodness) is not always connected with beauty, and, what is called enlightenment experience (Nirvana, Samadhi) becomes inescapably connected with interpretations which are irreconcilable.

Methodological doubt of ordinary (or extra-ordinary) experience led Descartes to what he took to be the first and indubitable truth of reason (I think, therefore I am), upon which he attempted to erect a superstructure of knowledge (foundationalism). But the *Cogito ("I think")* became doubted in light of monism (absolute idealism) along with the mind/body and subject/object distinctions. The existence of the self is no more self-evident than the existence of God ("We hold these truths to be self-evident, that all men are created equal"). Furthermore, the traditional proofs for the existence of God (ontological, cosmological, and teleological), taken separately, were found problematic at least, over a period of time. And reason seemed to present us with equally coherent and incommensurable worlds (Leibniz and Spinoza). Kant's synthesis of sense experience and reason left the world beyond appearance (the noumenal world) devoid of cognizable content and open to the speculation which followed. Reason, with its tendency to universalize, was seen as incapable of grasping the particulars of the real world (Nietzsche), or the concrete situation in which all exists (Kierkegaard).

Far from reason being a transcendent standard which gives knowledge of an objective world in which we exist, hermeneutical skepticism holds that reason (as well as science) is itself subject to the situation in which we find ourselves. We are always historically situated and cannot transcend our history. The world we live in is constructed on the basis of our identities and language grounded in our social context. There is no objective world in itself (anti-realism). The canons of rationality differ from one worldview to another. All is interpretation (Nietzsche). We are bound in a hermeneutical circle. Claims to objectivity are attempts to privilege one's own position for advantage over others. It is inevitably repressive of the other, in the name of common standard, defined by one's own meta-narrative. Since all things are understood within the confines of one's meta-narrative, one must recognize incommensurability between worldviews, the reality of alterity, and the ultimacy of difference. This recognition is said to be the virtue of tolerance. Hermeneutical skepticism says our beliefs are inescapably without proof and should be recognized as such. Fideism acquiesces to this.

Fideism

Fideism applies to all interpretive belief systems which make no attempt to prove their first principles, especially in light of existing challenges to them. It applies to theism as well as to anti-theism, to science as well as to philosophy, to realism as well as to anti-realism, to foundationalism as well as to anti-foundationalism. It occurs whenever reasons given are not sufficient to rationally exclude competing views. While fideism applies to a wide range of views, most discussions have focused on theistic fideism, particularly on Christian fideism. Christians have attempted to give reasons for their beliefs, but, in light of the challenges of skepticism, Christian fideism has responded by maintaining either reason (proof) is not necessary for belief or not sufficient for belief or not called for by scripture.

That reason (proof) is not necessary for belief in God seems obvious since many believe without proof. Many maintain that faith, by definition, is not sight (proof) and many have no idea of the proofs which have been given historically. Some have argued that reason is not necessary since belief in God is properly basic, like belief in the external world, for which proof seems irrelevant. Properly basic beliefs occur naturally under certain conditions if one's cognitive faculties are properly functioning. Natural belief in God is warranted, without proof, although warrant may be weakened in the presence of objections if they are unanswered (Plantinga). Again, reason is said to be unnecessary for faith since faith is said to precede understanding and that we must believe in order that we might understand. Having first believed, faith then seeks to understand (Augustine). And again, reason is said to be unnecessary since faith is by grace and not a work of human reason (Barth).

Furthermore, reason is said to be insufficient for faith. The proofs do not seem to persuade most people to believe, nor does knowing move someone to act. People are said to know, deep down, the truth of God's existence and yet suppress this truth, and to know what is right and yet do what is wrong. Reason is said to be finite and incapable of discovering or apprehending the mysteries of the faith, which remain paradoxes to the intellect, even after they are made known by revelation. If some are able to come to the truth of first things through dialectic, this is not available to most (Plato's Allegory of the Cave), and is accessible only to few minds which have been trained in metaphysics (Aquinas). Faith is said to be inaccessible to reason. The individual before God, in his unique particularity (Abraham called to sacrifice Isaac), has no guidance possible from reason which deals in universals. Faith is a leap beyond reason (Kierkegaard). Reason is said to be fallen and fallible and its use, apart from revelation, leads man away from God. Reason is said to be conditioned by pretheoretical commitments so that all proofs are in the end circular, reflecting one's presupposition. And lastly, reason itself is said to be not sufficient for justification but is thought to itself require justification, which can be found only in God, specifically, in the triune God of the Bible (Van Til/Bahnsen).

There are reasons offered for fideism based on appeal to scripture. There are no proofs given in scripture for the existence of God so it is thought that no proof is necessary. This view assumes that everything needed by the believer is expressly given in scripture, and in a form that does not require good and necessary consequences. This view affirms the sole authority of scripture (*sola scriptura*) over and against all other authorities, including reason and general revelation, not merely over all other appeals to special revelation and to persons as authorities. It is pointed out that there are warnings raised in scripture against the wisdom of this world, and against vain philosophy (*simpliciter*). There is said to be in scripture an exaltation of proclamation of things foolish in the eyes of the world, and this is understood in a way that excludes reasoning and persuasion. Furthermore, the fullness of blessing is said to be reserved for those faithful in this life who will, in life after death, see God face to face (beatific vision). The highest good therefore does not require and is not accessible to the life of reason.

The Necessity for Natural Theology

One response to the pressing weight of skepticism and fideism is to make the point that the knowledge of God (and of the world) is not discursive, to be attained by reason and inference. It is more akin to knowledge by experience through acquaintance or encounter. It cannot be expressed in words or communicated to another through words. One must have the experience. This knowledge is non-cognitive (not a matter of true or false), and non-propositional (not to be argued for or against). It is immediate, direct, personal, relational, and mystical, like an embrace.

While it is true enough that thinking is not the same as or a substitute for experience, it is equally the case that experience is not the same as or a substitute for thinking. They are two distinct but inseparable aspects of human knowledge. We don't simply experience but "experience as." An embrace has significance in light of assumptions about the other in the embrace, assumptions not derived from the experience itself, assumptions of which we may become more conscious and critical and perhaps change, so that the significance of the embrace may change or deepen over time in one and the same person. No experience is meaningful without interpretation. Any appeal to experience stripped of interpretation becomes meaningless. The shift to non-cognitivism in order to possess knowledge, without engaging with the objections of skepticism and fideism, and without engaging in natural theology, is in vain since experience devoid of meaning is empty. A different strategy is required which can show the inadequacy of both skepticism and fideism, even as non-cognitivism is inadequate.

Skepticism has value. Its value is negative. Its lasting value is that it will not let fideism pass without identifying itself as such. Skepticism is aware of the arbitrariness of fideism when it claims to be objective and exclusive, and finds that arbitrariness self-destructive. But skepticism reaches an over-extended conclusion (that no knowledge is possible) by assuming it has considered all relevant assumptions. There are assumptions, however, which skepticism has not considered. There are alternatives to the assumption of monism (either nothing is eternal or all is eternal). There are alternatives to ontological dualism (both matter and spirit are eternal). Theism, the view that only some (God the creator) is eternal is an alternative to both monism and dualism. There are alternatives to rationalism and to empiricism and to the synthesis of the two, which recognize what is uncritically assumed in both. There are alternatives to science (pure facts without interpretation) and deconstruction (pure interpretation without facts). One can identify and distinguish pure experience/fact (for example, the embrace) from its significance, given by interpretation. If there were no alternatives to the assumptions it has considered, then skepticism would be granted. But if it were granted, and carried out consistently, skepticism would lead to hopelessness and nihilism, the destruction of all meaning by the destruction of all distinctions. Qualified skepticism ("this view is incoherent") is possible; total skepticism ("all views are incoherent") becomes self-referentially absurd.

Fideism, too, has value, and its value is positive. It recognizes the impossibility of nihilism to which skepticism leads, and the inadequacy of pragmatism to overcome self-conscious nihilism. Positions of fideism purport to offer its adherents a meaningful vision of the world. A more self-conscious fideism maintains its right to exist by an exclusivist claim to truth and meaning. But fideism wishes to make some distinction between faith and understanding. In the motto "faith seeking understanding" it is assumed that one can believe more than one understands. If it were possible to believe more than one understands then one could believe what one did not understand. To open a gap between believing p to be true and understanding p is to affirm p while emptying p of meaning. I believe p as far as I understand p. There is more to understand of p, and I seek to understand more of p but I do not and cannot believe more than I understand. If "faith seeking understanding" means "understanding seeking more understanding" there is nothing controversial here. By faith I believe p to be true; by reason I understand the meaning of p. As truth is inseparable from meaning so faith is inseparable from reason. It is not the case that faith is static and understanding grows in "faith seeking understanding." Faith grows as understanding grows; faith is tested as understanding is tested.

Faith, in the theistic sense, is directed to what is invisible. Faith is contrasted with sight, which is directed to the visible, but it is not contrasted with understanding which is directed to what is invisible. Faith in Christian theism is being sure of what is hoped for and certain of what is not seen (Hebrews 11). Since faith is inseparable from understanding, the certainty of faith is the certainty of understanding. The certainty of understanding in faith is not different from the certainty of understanding a proof for what is unseen. Fideism, therefore, insofar as it separates faith and understanding, empties faith of meaning and nullifies its purpose, which is to offer its adherents a meaningful vision of the world. But insofar as it does not separate faith and understanding, it has the certainty of proof in its understanding. So true faith, contrary to fideism, is inseparable from reason, understanding, certainty, and proof. Faith, without reason and proof, that is, fideism, is empty of meaning. Fideism fails in the same way that skepticism fails. Both fail to preserve meaning. Both failures make natural theology necessary.

There is a third set of reasons why natural theology is necessary. Historic Christianity is structured on the theme of Creation, Fall, and Redemption. The implications of each of these, when understood, requires NT. Historic Christianity assumes the reality of sin. Since sin is a reality in Christianity, Christianity must give some account of sin. Unbelief is regarded as root sin. Unbelief is inexcusable because there is a clear general revelation of the existence and nature of God in the creation. "For since the creation of the world His invisible *attributes* are clearly seen, being understood by the things that are made, *even* His eternal power and Godhead, so that they are without excuse (Romans 1:20)." Men are without excuse for unbelief of what is clear. If there is no clarity of general revelation for which one is held accountable there can be no sin. But if there is clarity of general revelation then presumably one should be able to see what is clear. And since it is clear one should be able to show what is clear, especially over and against objections which would deny clarity. To see what is clear is to see why the denial of clarity fails. Christian theists, believing in the reality of sin, should be able to show what is clear. To do so would be to do natural theology.

Historic Christianity not only affirms the reality of sin but it affirms divine judgment on sin. The wages of sin is death (Romans 6). This death is present in unbelief in this life and in the life to come. This death is spiritual and is inherent in unbelief. It is the meaninglessness that is inherent in the failure to see what is clear at the most basic level of all of one's understanding. This death is also said to be everlasting. Everlasting death is maximal consequence. Maximal consequence requires maximal inexcusability, which in turn requires maximal clarity. The contradiction of what is maximally clear is not logically possible. Maximal clarity can be avoided only by ceasing to think, that is, giving-up or denying reason itself. Natural theology in Christian theism must show maximal clarity.

Historic Christianity affirms redemption. Christ is the Lamb of God who takes away the sin of the world. If sense is to be made of the death of Christ by which sin and death are removed, then clarity and inexcusability must be shown by natural theology.

Historic Christianity has been exclusivist, believing that redemption is through Christ alone. It also believes that Christ's redemption is for all peoples. If people are called away from competing worldviews to the Christian world-view, reasons for the truth of its exclusive claims which do not beg the question must be given. This requires natural theology.

Historic Christianity holds up the highest good and the goal of life as the knowledge of God. Creation and history reveal God. Through an age-long and agonizing spiritual war good will overcome evil. The earth shall be full of the knowledge of God as the waters cover the sea. If God's justice and mercy are to be understood, the inexcusability of unbelief must be understood. If we do not understand clarity then we cannot understand inexcusability. But if we understand clarity then we can show clarity. This is the work of natural theology.

What is Reason and Clarity?

Throughout this book the term "clarity" has been used, often in connection to "reason." What is clear, is clear to reason and is therefore objectively clear, as opposed to being personally/subjectively clear. The best way to define "clarity" is to give an example: it is clear that "a" is not "non-a." This is maximal clarity, which is necessary for maximal responsibility. If humans are maximally responsible before God for seeking, understanding, and doing what is right then there must be this kind of clarity of about God's existence and nature. For instance, if humans are responsible for knowing that only God is eternal, then it must be clear that connecting "eternal" with "non-God" (matter, a finite spirit, some combination of the two) is a contradiction.

Some clarification in the understanding of reason is necessary in order to show more specifically how knowledge is possible. There are different senses of reason that must be kept clearly in mind whenever the term "reason" and its derivatives are used. There is first, reason in itself, to be distinguished from reason in its use and reason in us. There are different uses of reason and different aspects of reason in us.

Reason in itself is the laws of thought. These laws are most basically the law of identity (a is a), the law of non-contradiction (something cannot be both a and non-a in the same respect and the same time), and the law of excluded middle (something is either a or non-a). These, minimally, have been commonly accepted in the history of philosophy as the laws of reason and the laws of thought. "Finite" and "fallen" may apply to human users of these laws but not to the laws themselves. They may apply to the failure to use reason critically rather than a failure of reason itself. When any of these laws are broken reason is not being used and thinking ceases.

Reason is used to form concepts, judgments, and arguments which are the forms of all thought. Reason is used critically as a test of meaning. Meaning is more basic than truth. We must know what a statement means before we can know if it is true. When a law of thought is violated there is no meaning. Reason is used to interpret experience in light of one's basic beliefs. And reason is used constructively to construct a coherent world and life view. The constructive use of reason is not the same as the critical use. Reason should be used critically first to test one's basic beliefs for meaning, before constructing a worldview upon them. Likewise, the interpretive use must be distinguished from the critical use. Much confusion in hermeneutical skepticism can be avoided by observing some of these distinctions.

Reason in itself is natural, not conventional. It is universal, the same in all persons. It is a common ground between all worldviews. It is the source of coherence in constructing a worldview and in the test for meaning of its basic beliefs. It is the common ground by which thoughts (concepts, judgments, and arguments) are formed and that by which experience is interpreted in light of basic beliefs. Reason in itself as common ground is not historically situated; it is universal. This prevents incommensurability between worldviews, even when basic beliefs in different worldviews are contradictory.

Reason is ontological. It applies to being as well as to thought. There are no square-circles, no uncaused events, no being from non-being. God is not both eternal and not eternal in the same respect and at the same time. If reason did not apply to being then statements could be true and not true in the same respect and at the same time. If *a* could be *non-a*, then being could not be distinguished from non-being. All distinctions would lose meaning, and all meaning would be lost.

Reason is transcendental. It is authoritative. It is self-attesting, the highest authority. It cannot be questioned because it makes questioning possible. A statement which violates a law of reason is not meaningful and cannot be true, regardless of its source.

Reason is also fundamental. It is fundamental to other aspects of human personality. Thought supplies the belief concerning the good as the object of desire. And thought and desire move a person to act. It is knowing the truth that sets a person free.

Thinking is presuppositional. This follows from the nature of reason in itself, reason in its use and reason in us. We think of what is less basic in light of what is more basic. We think of truth in light of meaning; we think of experience in light of basic belief; we think of conclusion in light of premises; we think of the temporal in light of the eternal, and the finite in light of the infinite. We must know what a statement means before we can know if it is true. If it violates a law of reason it is not meaningful because reason, as the laws of thought, is transcendental—it is the test for meaning, and thus of what can and cannot be true. If a statement is meaningless it cannot be true because reason is ontological. If there is agreement on what is more basic (that reason is the laws of thought, universal, ontological, and transcendental) there can be agreement on what is less basic. If there is doubt that reason is ontological, disagreement is not even possible because skepticism here lapses into nihilism and the loss of meaning.

Since thinking is presuppositional, and reason, as the test for meaning, is most basic, this position can be described as rational presuppositionalism. It is a position distinct from empiricism, rationalism, and fideistic presuppositionalism.

First Application of Rational Presuppositionalism

The first application of Rational Presuppositionalism: show there must be something eternal. The first act of reason is in forming concepts, and the most basic concept is about existence. Since existence is either temporal (with beginning) or eternal (without beginning), and since eternal is more basic than temporal, our most basic concept is about eternal existence. The possible judgments concerning what is eternal are four: all is eternal; none is eternal; some is eternal; and some is not eternal. Can we know if there is something eternal? The following is offered as proof that something must be eternal:

1. Contradictory statements cannot both be true and both be false.
2. The contradiction of "some is eternal" is "none is eternal."
3. If nothing is eternal then:
    a. All is temporal.
    b. All had a beginning.
    c. All came into being.
    d. If all came into being then being came into existence from non-being.
    e. Being from non-being is not possible.
    f. Therefore the original "none is eternal" is not possible.
    g. Therefore its contradictory "some is eternal" must be true.

Being comes from being alone. Non-being is the absence of being and of the power of being to cause to be. If being could come from non-being then there would be no distinction between being and non-being ("*a*" could be "*non-a*"). Skepticism and nihilism would be the result.

It is clear through reason therefore that something must be eternal. To doubt this one must give up reason. To give up reason is to give up meaning. "There must be something eternal" is maximally clear. The opposite is not possible. To doubt what is maximally clear one must give up reason. To give up reason is to deny one's nature as a rational being and so to bring upon oneself spiritual death, which is meaninglessness.

The Program of Natural Theology

The goal of NT is to show what is clear about God and man and good and evil from general revelation. It is to respond to all objections raised against the knowledge of God, proceeding from what is most basic in general revelation to what is equally basic in special revelation. It must show all that is clear from general revelation (which is necessary for inexcusability), as well as respond to philosophical objections to the doctrines of special revelation. What follows is an outline of the objectives by which this goal is to be achieved. The objectives state what must be done and indicate only in the most general way how this may be done.

1. Show that there must be something eternal. Since eternal is our most basic concept and since God is eternal, it must be shown that there must be something eternal. This first step is necessary but not sufficient to prove the existence of God. This proof is a modification of the ontological argument: what cannot be logically conceived cannot exist.

2. Show that only some is eternal. Since God is creator of all things, only some (God) is eternal. All else is temporal. This step uses the cosmological argument in a variety of ways.

3. The material world is not eternal (vs. material monism). It is not self-maintaining in general (entropy), nor in its parts (sun and stars), nor as a whole (the big bang oscillating universe or the inflationary universe).

4. The material world exists (vs. ordinary idealism—Berkeley). The cause of what I see is not my mind, nor another mind, but outside all minds.

5. The soul exists—the mind is not the brain (vs. material monism). A neural impulse is not a mental image, nor does the mental image perceive itself.

6. The soul is not eternal (vs. ordinary dualism—Plato, and qualified non-dualism—Ramanuja). The soul goes through unique events in time (growth in knowledge, enlightenment, etc.).

7. The soul exists (vs. absolute idealism, Advaita—Shankara). The soul is neither unreal, that is, an illusion/maya, nor real/eternal).

8. Respond to the problem of evil. If God is all good and all powerful why is there evil? The teleological argument is used to respond to the problem of natural evil and moral evil.
    a. Natural evil (toil, strife, old age, sickness and death) is not necessary. Original creation was very good, without natural evil (vs. origin by evolution, natural or theistic).
    b. Natural evil is due to moral evil. It is imposed, not as punishment, but as a call back from moral evil. Suffering is a call to stop and think.

    c.   Moral evil is permitted for a purpose; it is made to serve the good through deepening of the divine revelation.

    d.   There is an ironic solution to the problem of evil, requiring understanding the nature of evil in light of the clarity of general revelation.

9.   Show the moral law from general revelation. If there is not a moral law which is clear from general revelation then human responsibility and moral evil are not possible. This moral law must be clear, comprehensive, and critical.

    a.   The moral law is clear because it is grounded in the fundamental features of human nature. It is grounded in the reality of choice, in the nature of thinking, in the natural unity of our being, in the work required to bring into being and sustain in being, in being born ignorant, in being born human, in being born of a sexual union, in valuing and producing what is of value, in being born equal, in being born changeable.

    b.   The moral law is comprehensive in that it applies to all choices and all aspects of human nature which come to expression in choice.

    c.   The moral law is critical. The consequence of observing the moral law is life, which is, obtaining the good; the consequence of not observing the law is spiritual death, both individual and corporate.

10.   From deism to theism.

    a.   Deism maintains that God creates but does not act in history.

    b.   Theism (Judaism, Christianity, and Islam) maintains that God creates and acts providentially in history including, specifically, in giving scriptures.

    c.   God acts in history in imposing natural evil. Natural evil was not in the original creation and is not inherent in moral evil.

    d.   Natural evil as a call back from moral evil requires redemptive revelation to show how God can be both just and merciful.

    e.   Special revelation must be consistent with general revelation and must show how God is both just and merciful.

    f.   Biblical revelation only is consistent with general revelation and shows how God is both just and merciful.

11.   The root of conflict among theists.

    a.   Judaism, Christianity, and Islam profess to hold to some basic scriptures in common. Since scripture is redemptive revelation, the conflict between them is rooted in their understanding of the divine nature regarding how God is both just and merciful in redemption.

    b.   Judaism and Christianity affirm that God is both just and merciful by nature and that mercy must satisfy divine justice by atonement. Islam affirms that God has no nature by which he is bound; mercy can set aside divine justice—there is no need for atonement.

    c.   Biblical Judaism affirms the justice and mercy of God in vicarious atonement through the death of another as seen in the Temple sacrifice on the Day of Atonement. Post-biblical Judaism affirms that atonement is in and by oneself.

    d.   Christianity affirms the justice and mercy of God in vicarious atonement through human representation (Christ in the place of Adam). The lamb symbolically represented Christ, in whose death the reality of atonement is accomplished.

12. Rational challenges to doctrines of Christianity. Non-theists and non-Christian theists have objected to ecumenical doctrines in Christianity. If scripture is divine revelation it must be shown that these doctrines, while not originating from human reasoning, are in accordance with reason and are consistent with all that can be expected from both general and special revelation.

    a.   The doctrine of the Trinity requires an understanding of what is meant in saying "God is one."

    b.   The doctrine of the Incarnation requires an understanding of unity and diversity of two natures in one person.

    c.   The doctrine of the Fall requires an understanding of the nature of moral evil (sin) and of representation.

13. Philosophical questions in the continuing divisions within Christianity. Redemptive revelation in scripture assumes the reality of sin as seen in the failure to understand clear general revelation. Understanding scripture assumes the understanding of general revelation. Continuing divisions within Christianity reveal lack in understanding what is clear in general revelation. The perspicuity of scripture rests on the clarity of general revelation.

    a.   There is continuing division concerning the sufficiency of vicarious atonement (grace vs. works).

    b.   There is continuing division concerning divine sovereignty in predestination and human freedom and responsibility.

    c.   There is continuing division concerning hermeneutics: what is literal and what is contextual interpretation, and what is the order within contextual layers.

    d.   There is continuing division concerning the good: is the knowledge of God gained through a direct vision of God in heaven or is it the knowledge of God gained through the work of dominion on earth through history?

Jonathan Edwards and John Locke

These steps state very clearly the challenges that must be addressed and the manner in which to proceed with natural theology.[1] To some extent such steps have been noticed before. For instance, consider the following questions asked by Jonathan Edwards of his theology students:

1. How does it appear that something has existed from eternity?
2. How does it appear that this earth and the visible system are not from eternity?
3. How does it appear that the existence of man is derived and dependent?
4. How do you prove the natural perfections of God, *viz.* his intelligence, infinite power, foreknowledge, and immutability?
5. How do you prove his moral perfection, that he is a friend of virtue, or absolutely holy, true, just, and good?
6. How do you prove that the scriptures are a revelation from God? And what are the evidences, internal and external?
7. How do you prove the divine mission of Christ?[2]

This follows a pattern set by John Locke. Locke asserted that humans are capable of being certain that there is a God, indeed with a certainty second only to their own existence.[3] Furthermore, he denies that humans have an intuitive idea of God, but instead argues that humans require a proof. The first step in this proof is to show that being cannot come from non-being: "If therefore we know there is some real Being, and that Non-entity cannot produce any real Being, it is an evident demonstration, that from Eternity there has been something; Since what was not from Eternity, had a Beginning; and what had a Beginning, must be produced by something else."[4] He then continues to argue for the clarity of the nature of God.

Locke also maintained that what is found in special revelation cannot be a self-contradiction or contradict what is known from general revelation by reason.[5] Special revelation is necessary not to go beyond reason, but to communicate truths not discoverable by reason.[6] Locke gives as examples that some angels fell from grace, and the resurrection of the dead. His intention is making the distinction between reason and faith in special revelation is to help avoid vain disputes like those of the Religious Wars. His plan is that these can be avoided by coming to agreement on what can be known by reason from general revelation, and rejecting any interpretation of special revelation that involves a contradiction or the setting aside of reason.

It is evident both in England and the United States that the plan of natural theology given by Locke and Edwards did not help avoid divisions within Christianity, or between Christianity and other religions. Nor did it result in a general agreement about the clarity of God's existence. Why not? Locke himself noted the absurdities to be found in religion and gave an early statement of the judgment that Modernity will pass on religious belief:

For Men having been principled with an Opinion, that they must not consult *Reason* in the Things of Religion, however apparently contradictory to common Sense, and the very Principles of all their Knowledge, have let loose their Fancies, and natural Superstition; and have been, by them, led into so strange Opinions, and extravagant Practices in Religion, that a considerate Man cannot but stand amazed at their Follies, and judge them so far from being acceptable to the great and wise GOD, that he cannot avoid thinking them ridiculous, and offensive to a sober, good Man. So that, in effect Religion which should most distinguish us from Beasts, and ought most peculiarly to elevate us, as rational Creatures, above Brutes, is that wherein Men often appear most irrational, and more senseless than Beasts themselves.[7]

The temptation will be to say that Edwards and Locke were correct and people simply did not listen. There is something to this, but it does not answer the question because it does not explain why people did not listen. The answer cannot be that people are not intelligent enough to understand because then they cannot be held responsible for unbelief. Nor can the answer be that they are distracted by other concerns because that simply raises the question "why are they distracted by other concerns instead of being concerned about what is clear about God?" This does hint at the answer in that it is connected with what people are interested in as a source of fulfillment and joy. The answer can be found in ways in which both Edwards and Locke came short in explaining the need for a clear general revelation. Edwards is communicating this to advanced theology students, and Locke to those who read his *Essay*, but what about the vast majority of people? Do they need to know what is clear about God, and if so why?

Neither of these thinkers saw the necessity for natural theology or provided a foundation for natural theology that lasted against challenges. Edwards is best known for his sermon "Sinners in the Hand of an Angry God." While this clearly presents the reality of sin and death, and the need for atonement, did Edwards also explain that this atonement restores the believer to seeking and understanding? Or is this theology ultimately focused on going to heaven? If the need is for justification to go to heaven and there find the blessing and fulfillment, what is the need for the work of natural theology (which is often laborious and difficult)? Edwards's concern in the First Great Awakening was with an inner experience and excitement about salvation that gave witness to the work of the Holy Spirit in the life of the person. But the work of the Holy Spirit restores a person to seeking and understanding (not only to doing what is right—as if these could be divided). Thus, full evidence of this work is not only in personal testimony about experiences, but in being able to show that one is seeking and understand.

Locke had similar shortcomings. While he argues against irrationality and enthusiasm in religion, his understanding of scripture is that God gave a law which humans must keep in order to attain immortality and Paradise, the breach of which leads to death.[8] Locke held that the essence of Christianity is those truths that are found in scripture and necessary to be believed in order to have eternal salvation in heaven.[9] This builds on Locke's view of the original state of man in Paradise; before the Fall Adam lived in a continual state of bliss, tranquility, and immortality.[10] He was threatened with death if he ate the fruit, and although he did not die physically when he ate, he was cast out of Paradise which is a death that is then passed to his children. Here, life is viewed as bliss, tranquility, and immortality, death as the lost of these. Indeed, Locke's view of eternal life appears simply to mean immortality. But is this enough to motivate persons to seek and understand, if they can achieve eternal life through belief and justification? Is the goal of the Christian life bliss and tranquility? Or are these effects of achieving the goal which is to seek and understand God? Is death the loss of immortality, or is death the loss of life, eternal life being the knowledge of God (John 17:3)? If blessedness resides in knowing God, and this requires seeking and understanding, then Locke did not provide a firm foundation for natural theology. Locke's failure to explain these issues, and his mistakes about Paradise, life and death, provided ground for objections to the clarity of general revelation, beginning with David Hume and continuing to the present.

Conclusion

Natural Theology has been neglected (even rejected), and yet it is necessary for the most basic claims of Christianity to make sense. In his book, *The Outrageous Idea of Christian Scholarship*, George Marsden notes that there is a new revival of work by Christian philosophers, but then names persons like Alvin Plantinga and Nicholas Wolterstorff as examples. These persons, both involved with Reformed Epistemology, downplay the need for NT. At best there is a reassertion of the warrant of being a Christian and pursuing an academic career, and possibly a resurrection of the traditional theistic proofs. But the focus is different. The focus is not on showing the clarity of God's existence as opposed to alternative worldviews. Consequently, what is a non-Christian to think about this development? If Christianity is based on redemptive claims, but cannot prove that there is a failure to seek and understand, then what does this say about the coherence of the Christian worldview? Were the Princeton Theologians, such as Hodge and Warfield, on to something in their view of reason? Can their mistakes about Common Sense Realism be corrected? And what caused this mistake? Could it have been a focus on heaven rather than the knowledge of God? These questions arise as we consider the program of NT and its possibilities.

Questions:
1.   What is natural theology? Why is it necessary?
2.   What are clarity, reason, skepticism, fideism?
3.   Why must there be something eternal?
4.   What is required to show that only some is eternal?
5.   What is required to show that the soul exists but is not eternal?
6.   What is required to respond to the problem of evil?
7.   What is required to move from deism to theism?
8.   What are some remaining conflicts between theists?
9.   What are some rationalist challenges to Christianity?

10. What are some remaining conflicts within Christianity?
11. What steps did Jonathan Edwards and John Locke give to prove that God exists?
12. How did Edwards and Locke come short of providing a firm foundation for natural theology? Why did this happen, and how can it be corrected?

CHAPTER 8: CONCLUSION

Can the challenges to Christianity be responded to by simply reformulating the traditional apologetic methods and theistic proofs, or do these challenges reveal inadequacies in these that must be answered? Why continue to hold to the Christian message of redemption rather than abandon it in favor of the solutions given by Modernity?

This book has examined B.B. Warfield's view of apologetics, his context at Princeton, his debate with Kuyper, and his legacy at Westminster Theological Seminary. The assumptions concerning inexcusability, clarity, and rationality that are behind Warfield's apologetic were examined in order to bring his view into focus and contrast it with Kuyper, Van Til and Plantinga. Warfield's view of right reason provides apologetics with the necessary components of inexcusability and clarity. In contrast, the systems of Kuyper, Van Til and Plantinga do not explain the need for clarity and rationality to establish inexcusability and therefore minimize the role of apologetics and bring rationality itself into question. While there are aspects of Warfield's system that may need closer attention, or even parts that appear problematic, his affirmation of right reason and the ability for all persons at all times to know God makes sense of inexcusability and redemption in a way that other systems do not. If there are failings in Warfield's view it is particularly with respect to being underdeveloped in these areas.

The focus has been on the knowledge of God because of the Christian claim that the failure to know God is inexcusable. However, this book has not looked at Warfield's actual proofs for God's existence. It makes sense to conclude by giving a brief summary of Warfield's view of the knowledge of God and consider some possible problems and questions remaining to be answered. Of the knowledge of God's existence, Warfield said that there is an intuitive knowledge of God which is both universal and unavoidable.[1] This truth is given in the very same act as the idea of self, because the self is dependent and implies one on whom it is dependent. This immediate perception of God is supported by the theistic proofs.[2] These proofs give us not only God's existence but also his nature as a personal Spirit, who is infinite and eternal, and having properties such as power, knowledge, wisdom, righteousness, holiness, and goodness.[3]

Problems for Warfield

There are three possible problems in Warfield's approach to the knowledge of God. First, the idea of God's existence as an intuitive truth is unclear and ultimately not helpful in establishing inexcusability. Second, whether this approach, often called evidentialism, can provide certainty or only probability. Third, his reliance on the theistic proofs in light of substantial challenges to these raised by David Hume and Immanuel Kant.

Sensus Divinitatis

The idea of an intuitive knowledge of God, an immediate knowledge of God, or the *sensus divinitatis*, is the claim that everybody has some knowledge of God naturally and unavoidably. Unbelief is thus viewed as an attempt to avoid what is unavoidable. Those who hold this position sometimes tell nontheists that they really do believe in God but are not acknowledging this belief. The problem with this is that the knowledge that everyone is supposed to have of God is either not universal, or extremely vague. It is easy to prove that not everybody has a knowledge or belief in God as defined by theism (a spirit, infinite, eternal, and unchanging in power, knowledge, goodness, etc.). It does not follow that because humans are dependent on another being that this other being is God in the theistic sense of that term. Theistic belief has not been held by every human throughout history, nor is it held by every human alive today. To assert that the *sensus divinitatis* is a much more general knowing of God, more like a higher power or greater other, is to concede that the idea of God is not known intuitively because God is not merely a higher power or greater other. Nor is it sufficient to affirm that all humans have worshiped something and that this "something" counts as the *sensus divinitatis*. The actual object of worship, for example Zeus, Baal, Thor, et. al., is very different from God. And yet Romans 1:20 affirms that God's eternal power and divine nature are knowable so that ignorance of these is inexcusable.

It is the eternal power and divine nature of God, not a vague sense of a higher power, that Paul says is knowable and the ignorance of which is inexcusable (Romans 1:20). And when Paul says that God's existence and nature are known *from* the things that are made this suggests an inference, not an immediate or intuitive truth. When Paul says in verse 21 that "although they knew God, they did not glorify Him as God, nor were thankful, but became futile in their thoughts, and their foolish hearts were darkened" (NKJV), there seems to be a progression from having known God to failing to know God. It is far from clear that the word "they" in this passage refers to all humans who have ever lived, but rather may be referring to an original context where humans knew God, and then a process wherein humanity exchanged belief in God for belief in idols.

Further, non-theists can make a similar claim about their belief. It is easy to assert that "deep down" everyone really believes the truth. The problem with such a claim for Christianity is that it does not maintain that unbelief is inexcusable because there is no unbelief since everyone believes intuitively. But the inexcusability of unbelief, in the failure to know God's eternal power and divine nature from the things that have been made, is a central part of Romans 1. In terms of Old Princeton and Warfield, the claim that God's existence is known intuitively may be an effect of Reid's Common Sense Philosophy. As was noted in Chapter One, many of the truths that this philosophy claims are known through common sense are in fact disputed and require proof. God's existence is one such example. A related claim is that a person is within his/her "epistemic rights" to believe in God without proof. This is a different claim altogether than that all humans have an intuitive idea of God, although both may have been influenced by Reid. To establish that a given person is within his/her epistemic rights does not establish that unbelief is inexcusable and requires redemption through Christ. To maintain that unbelief requires redemption it is necessary to establish that unbelief is inexcusable.

In Warfield, this problem was traced to his reliance on Augustine, and the latter's reliance on Platonism and how this affected his interpretation of Romans 13:13–14. If the blessed life is after death when we are released from the body, and the blessing comes from a direct vision of God apart from his work, then why should we seek to understand God through his work in this life? Why not be saved and wait to die and go to heaven and there receive the true blessing? This remnant of Platonism in Warfield undermined the other work he did on reason and apologetics. Today, Christians are very familiar with this view of heaven, but few have heard of Warfield's view of reason.

Evidentialism

A second problem in Warfield's method is that he, and Old School Princeton more generally, tended toward evidentialism. He seems to have taken this approach to establishing the veracity of the Bible. "This method, as we have seen, seeks to build upon the basis of adequate evidence *grounds* for the validity of the Christian faith prior to personal commitment."[4] Robert Reymond sees this method present in Warfield in the latter's argument for the inspiration of the Bible. Warfield said:

> We do not adopt the doctrine of the plenary inspiration of Scripture on sentimental grounds, nor even, as we have already had occasion to remark, on *a priori* or general grounds of whatever kind. We adopt it specifically because it is taught us as truth by Christ and His apostles, in the Scriptural record of their teaching, and the evidence for its truth is, therefore, as we have also already pointed out, precisely that evidence, in weight and amount, which vindicates

for us the trustworthiness of Christ and His apostles as teachers of doctrine. Of course, this evidence is not in the strict logical sense "demonstrative;" it is "probable" evidence. It therefore leaves open the metaphysical possibility of its being mistaken.[5]

Probability does not establish inexcusability. If the Bible could be mistaken, then unbelief cannot be said to be inexcusable. There is an excuse for not believing, namely, that a person believes one of the other alternatives that might be correct if the Bible is mistaken. "But evidence, at best, is *only probable* and, at worst, *meaningless* in the natural man's world where Chance is ultimate. . . . The evidentialist himself admits his case is *at best* a probable one. This approach leaves the man who refuses to regard the evidence as compelling with the delusion that the *best* basis the Christian can claim for his faith is a probable one."[6]

Both Kuyper and Van Til saw the problems in the evidential approach. They saw that what counts as evidence in one worldview may not count as evidence in another worldview. As was seen in previous chapters, their response was to assert that there is not neutral ground between the Christian and the non-Christian worldviews. What is evidence for the Christian will not count as evidence for the non-Christian. This is a very helpful insight, and it may be that Warfield failed to see this in using an evidentialist approach.

However, it is not clear that Warfield asserted that all aspects of the Christian worldview are only established on probability through the use of evidence. He does not seem to approach God's existence this way. He speaks of the necessity of belief in God, and that this can be established through proofs.[7] Perhaps there is a tension in Warfield on this point. His approach to God's existence appears to support the claim in Romans that unbelief is inexcusable. He affirms that reason is common ground for all humans, although it is not neutral because it leads to theism and finds a contradiction in non-theism. But something can be taken from Kuyper and Van Til by seeing that worldviews are logical systems that are proven or refuted by addressing their internal consistency, and the consistency of the presuppositions from which the entire worldview is derived. What must be established by apologetics is the inexcusability of non-theism as a worldview (or multiple different worldviews). Warfield affirms this can be done with respect to the existence of God, and perhaps it is left to others to take it further.

Hume, Kant and the Challenge to the Traditional Proofs

Finally, problems may arise for Warfield's method due to his reliance on the theistic proofs. These proofs received an important challenge by both David Hume and Immanuel Kant. This challenge has led many to conclude that God's existence cannot be proven. For instance, consider a passage from a recent book that claims to be a response to Hume and a defense of natural theology:

Two facts of contemporary philosophy leave Hume's legacy open to vigorous attack. The first concerns the revival in NT study mentioned above. This revival has largely been concerned with what we might call "modest NT." Contemporary philosophers of religion seldom claim a NT argument *proves* or *demonstrates* the existence of God, or even that it offers *overwhelming* evidence for it, such that no person aware of the argument's implications could rationally reject its conclusion.[8]

The authors go on to say that it is likely there is no philosophical proof that can give such a demonstration. Nothing is clear. If nothing is clear then how can persons be held responsible for not seeking? While these authors claim to be "vigorously attacking" Hume, they are uncritically accepting his assumptions about knowledge and faith, and unconsciously promoting them in their natural theology. Consider Hume's distinction between faith and reason:

> Our most holy religion is founded on *Faith*, not on reason; and it is a sure method of exposing it to put it to such a trial as it is, by no means, fitted to endure. . . . we may conclude, that the *Christian Religion* not only was at first attended with miracles, but even at this day cannot be believed by any reasonable person without one. Mere reason is insufficient to convince us of its veracity: And whoever is moved by *Faith* to assent to it, is conscious of a continued miracle in his own person, which subverts all the principles of his understanding, and gives him a determination to believe what is most contrary to custom and experience.[9]

And Hume's view of reason and the source of knowledge:

> All kinds of reasoning consist in nothing but a *comparison*, and a discovery of those relations, either constant or inconstant, which two or more objects bear to each other. This comparison we may make, either when both the objects are present to the senses, or when neither of them is present . . . According to this way of thinking, we ought not to receive as reasoning any of the observations we may make concerning *identity*, and the *relations* of time and *place*; since in none of them the mind can go beyond what is immediately present to the senses, either to discover the real existence or the relations of objects.[10]

According to Hume, all knowledge is through sense data.[11] He notes that mere assertion and fideism lead to violence, each side claiming to be warranted while holding the other inexcusable.

Hume begins his *Treatise* by noting in the introduction that no proof can be given for starting principles (ix), and that it is not reason that wins the day but eloquence (ix). Indeed, if we do not recognize our ignorance we attempt to persuade others through violence, which is always a failure (ix). It is because of this that Hume says he is against metaphysical reasonings of all kinds. If a work is found to contain such subjects it should be cast to the flames.

But did Hume go far enough? While questions can be raised about his limitations to knowledge, problems can be seen even within Hume's framework. If we accept that knowledge only comes from sense impressions and the relationship of ideas, can we agree with Hume that reason cannot demonstrate God's existence? I think here he reveals a failure to seek. The distinction between "eternal" and "non-eternal" is clear, and the claim that "the eternal is non-eternal" is clearly false (or meaningless). Hume recognizes that relating contradictory ideas is meaningless. Does he recognize that relating eternality to something that cannot be eternal (the material world, finite self, combination of the two) is meaningless? Even within Hume's constricting framework it can be shown that it is clear that only God is eternal. And yet Hume missed this, as have "defenders of the faith" since Hume. Why?

Kant's challenge is directed at all proof of God's existence, which he asserts ultimately rests on the ontological proof. "Thus the physico-theological proof [teleological proof] of the existence of an original or supreme being rests upon the cosmological proof, and the cosmological upon the ontological. And since, besides these three, there is no other path open to speculative reason, the ontological proof from pure concepts of reason is the only possible one, if indeed any proof of a proposition so far exalted above all empirical employment of the understanding is possible at all."[12] And the ontological proof, according to Kant, does not prove the existence of God.

> The concept of a supreme being is in many respects a very useful idea; but just because it is a mere idea, it is altogether incapable, by itself alone, of enlarging our knowledge in regard to what exists. . . . The attempt to establish the existence of a supreme being by means of the famous ontological argument of Descartes is therefore merely so much labour and effort lost; we can no more extend our stock of [theoretical] insight by mere ideas, than a merchant can better his position by adding a few noughts to his cash account.[13]

The central challenge present in Kant appears to be a challenge to reason and then to the theistic proofs. For such proofs to be successful reason must be able to tell us about existence. If it cannot do so, then the theistic proofs, and any proofs about what exists apart from sense experience, are unsound. This is an important challenge that must be addressed if theistic proofs are to be successful. It requires an examination and clarification about the nature of reason, especially in its ontological function in applying to both thought and being.

Kant can be objected to in the same way Hume was above. While questions can be raised about his distinction between the world-in-itself and the world as experienced, what about operating within his framework? He recognizes that contradictory ideas cannot be joined, or if they are the result is meaninglessness. Does he recognize that only God is eternal and the alternatives are meaningless? If so, what does this do to his objections about the move from thought to existence? If he continues to maintain that this proves nothing about the world-in-itself, but only about human ideas, then what can be known about the world-in-itself? Kant claims that nothing can be known about it, knowledge is only of sense impressions which are shaped by the human mind. But if nothing can be known about the world-in-itself, then nothing can be said about the world-in-itself, including that there is a world-in-itself. Consistency requires that Kant and Kantians remain silent about the world-in-itself. As far as human thought and discussion is concerned, there is only the world of sense impressions, and in this world claims that something is eternal, besides God, are meaningless.

Keeping in mind the need for clarity and the role of reason in distinguishing between "a" and "non-a," or "eternal" and "non-eternal," the challenge from Hume and Kant is imploded. By operating within the frameworks they provide, it still remains the case that self-contradictions are meaningless. Furthermore, their failure to follow their own systems to their logical conclusions about clarity, to consistently think about the implications of their epistemology on knowing God, is revelatory of the problem of not seeking and understanding.

Not Seeking, Not Understanding, Not Doing What is Right

How can the failure to explore clarity and inexcusability be explained? Why were thinkers at Princeton, like Hodge and Warfield, satisfied with common sense and the *sensus divinitatis*, even though they came close in other ways to giving a rational demonstration? Perhaps this can be understood by thinking about the goal that has been pursued by Christians. The Reformation began with a debate about the nature of justification, and since then both Protestants and Roman Catholics have agreed on the goal of the Christian life, going to heaven, although disagreeing about how to get there. If the goal of life is to go to heaven, and one can do this through profession and belief without proof, then what need is there for more? Perhaps some overactive intellectuals will look for more, but this can be treated as a hobby and is not necessary for the wider group. Not to mention that such intellectuals have often cut themselves off from the wider group and not made their work accessible or relevant. Indeed, the claim that NT is somehow important or necessary often elicits the reply: "You're saying I won't get into heaven if I can't prove that God exists?"

But what if the goal is not heaven, but knowing God?[14] Can God be known apart from seeking and understanding? And if this is the goal of the Christian life, and critics have shown that God cannot be known, then what happens to the Christian life and message? Or, on the other hand, if it is clear that God exists and life is knowing God, then why did Hume and Kant miss this? If, as notable and influential philosophers, they posed as seekers after wisdom, is it fair to ask them to show what is clear? And if their own systems can be shown to serve as a basis for clarity, but they missed this, what does this say about the extent to which they were seeking? Here I am asking more questions than I am answering, but I am doing so because they are the departure point from this book into further study. If Christianity maintains that humans should know God, and that the failure to know God is due to not seeking and understanding, then Christians should be able to show that it is clear that God exists so that unbelief is without excuse.

Challenges to belief in God have mounted since the Reformation. While the Westminster Confession of Faith begins by affirming the clarity of God's existence and nature, the challenge of Modernity has been directed at this claim. The continued failure to respond to this, or to respond in a minimal way that proves the existence of God but does not make knowing God the goal of the Christian life, had led to increased challenges and the inability for Christianity to make sense of its message. If it is clear that God exists, are Christians seeking this understanding as life itself, or is their concern to attain pleasures in heaven? Do Christians believe that they can bypass the need to seek by attaining direct/immediate knowledge of God in heaven without the work involved in seeking? If so, it is no wonder that little concern is placed on responding to the presuppositions behind the challenges in order to demonstrate clarity and encourage people to know God in all that by which he has made himself known.

The Alternative to Heaven

Throughout this book I have argued that one factor in the failure of Christianity to respond to challenges has been its view of heaven as the goal of life. In Christianity, heaven is the state after death but before the resurrection. For believers this is said to be a glorified state where sin is removed and they are with Christ. As we saw earlier, this is interpreted to be a direct, intuitive vision of God, and this beatific vision is thought by some to be the highest state of blessedness. We've already considered the shortcomings in this view, but is there an alternative? The problem is not in the ideas that after death the soul is conscious, believers are in a glorified state, and then comes the resurrection and the final judgment. The problem is the focus on the blessed state being a direct, intuitive vision of God or Christ. This view seems to be based on Platonism where the body is a hindrance to the perception of the forms. Christians replaced the forms with God. But is this the highest state, or is the highest state knowing God, which is an inferential knowledge that is called eternal life (John 17:3)? If this is the goal, then the hope in a direct vision of God is misplaced, and causes Christians to miss the many ways that God can be known. In this is a perpetuation of the problem of not seeking and understanding. If the goal is to know God in all that by which he makes himself known, and God cannot be seen directly (God is a spirit) but is known through his works, then this knowledge which is eternal life can be had now, and is continued after death, and is the same in essence as what will be had after the resurrection. To "see" Christ is not to understand Christ; a direct vision of Christ does not guarantee understanding. Eternal life as knowing God requires the work of responding to challenges and making inferences, as opposed to being saved and then waiting for heaven to attain a direct vision. Thus, the alternative to this version of heaven is eternal life, which his knowing God.

Conclusion

In his debate with Kuyper over apologetics, Warfield affirmed the necessity of establishing God's existence through rational argument in order to make sense of the Christian worldview. The claim that humans need redemption through Christ for their unbelief presupposes that unbelief is inexcusable. The purpose of this book has been to argue for the necessity of the inexcusability of unbelief within the Christian worldview, and argue that Warfield's approach to apologetics preserves this, in contrast to Kuyper, Van Til and Plantinga. However, it has also been seen that there is in Warfield a problem in his claim about intuitive knowledge of God, a possible tension due to evidentialist aspects of his approach, and more work to be done on the theistic proofs. This gives direction for further work in the area of apologetics and the question of the inexcusability of unbelief. Most importantly, we have seen that while challenges against belief in God have mounted, and Princeton began with the goal of training minister equipped to respond to these challenges, the goal of going to heaven has not proven to be a sufficient foundation to support the need for seeking and understanding. Replacing the goal of heaven with the goal of knowing God, a goal that can be sought in this life, the intermediate state of heaven, and after the resurrection, provides a foundation for establishing the necessity of natural theology. This necessity having been established, the clarity of general revelation and inexcusability of unbelief can be readily understood.

It is just such a foundation that is necessary. Earlier the work of Jonathan Edwards and John Locke was considered because both provide helpful steps in proving the existence of God, and both maintain that God's existence is certain and clear. And yet, since their time Christianity within England and the United States has failed to give a sufficient response to challenges, has divided into numerous sub-groups, and no longer continues to have the influence it did in their day. Their foundation was inadequate because it did not provide a sufficient motivation for natural theology; life was viewed as salvation and heaven rather than seeking and understanding God. If the challenges that have amassed are to be responded to in a way that is more than intellectual distraction, it must be as a result of a new foundational understanding of eternal life as knowing God. Warfield provides us with some help in this direction, but also contains mistakes that need to be addressed. Having considered Warfield's method, and the challenges to belief in God and the clarity of general revelation, we should now be in a better place to establish a foundation for the clarity of general revelation.

Questions:
1. What is the problem for Christians in appealing to the *sensus divinitatis*?
2. Why is evidentialism insufficient to establish clarity?
3. What is Hume's view of reason, knowledge and faith? Why did Hume reject metaphysical studies?
4. How can Hume be responded to from within his own system?

5. What is the central challenge from Kant against the theistic proofs?
6. How can Kant be responded to from within his own system?
7. Why might it be that Christians have not paid much attention to the need for clarity?
8. Is there immediate knowledge, or must knowledge be attained through the process of seeking and understanding?
9. What is a foundation?
10. What is the alternative to the common view of "heaven," why does the common view of heaven lead to not seeing the necessity to respond to challenges, and what, by way of contrast, is eternal life?

ENDNOTES

Chapter 1

1. Warfield, Benjamin Breckinridge. *Studies in Theology* (Grand Rapids: Baker Book House, 2000), 109.

2. Hoffecker, W. Andrew, "Benjamin B. Warfield," in *Reformed Theology in America*, ed. Wells, David (Grand Rapids: Baker Books, 1997), 65.

3. Audi, Robert, ed., *The Cambridge Dictionary of Philosophy* (Cambridge: Cambridge University Press, 1999), 822.

4. Kant argued that Reid failed to understand Hume's argument ("Prolegomena to Any Future Metaphysics" in *Modern Philosophy*, ed. by Forrest E. Baird and Walter Kaufmann (New Jersey: Prentice Hall, 1997), 532–602.

5. Reid, Thomas, "Essays on the Intellectual Powers of Man," in *Modern Philosophy*, ed. Forrest E. Baird and Walter Kaufmann (New Jersey: Prentice Hall, 1997), 484.

6. "The modern factors of historicism, sociology, and scientific method and outlook undercut the traditional views of the Bible, the supernatural, and any form of objective truth from beyond. Princeton Seminary and Warfield stood against these reinterpretations of reality, maintaining that there was a truth revealed to human beings from God" (McClanahan, James S, "Benjamin B Warfield: Historian of Doctrine in Defense of Orthodoxy 1881–1921," *Affirmation* 6 (Fall 1993): 89–111. 93.).

7. Warfield, "Introduction," in *Apologetics*, 26.

Chapter 2

1. Noll, Mark, "The Princeton Theology," *Reformed Theology in America*, ed. David Wells (Grand Rapids: Baker Books, 1997), 18.

2. Taylor, Marion Ann, *The Old Testament in the Old Princeton School (1812–1929)* (San Francisco: Mellen Research University Press, 1992), 6.

3. Taylor, *The Old Testament*, 7.

4. Taylor, *The Old Testament*, 8.

5. Taylor, *The Old Testament*, 8.

6. Taylor, *The Old Testament*, 9.

7. Taylor, *The Old Testament*, 9.

8. Taylor, *The Old Testament*, 9.

9. Taylor, *The Old Testament*, 11.

10. Warfield, Benjamin B. "Introduction," in *Apologetics*, Francis Beattie (Richmond: Presbyterian Committee of Publication, 1903), 19–32. 24

11. Noll, 21.

12. Noll, 22.

13. Marsden, George, *Understanding Fundamentalism and Evangelicalism* (Grand Rapids: Eerdmans Publishing Company, 1991), 128

14. Audi, 783.

15. Marsden, George, "The Collapse of American Evangelical Academia," in *Faith and Rationality: Reason and Belief in God*, ed. Alvin Plantinga and Nicholas Wolterstorff (Notre Dame: University of Notre Dame Press, 1983), 224.

16. Marsden, "The Collapse," 224.

17. Marsden, "The Collapse," 225.

18. Reid, "Essays," 483.

19. Reid, "Essays," 480.

20. Kant, "Prolegomena," 535.

21. Reid, "Essays," 483.

22. Marsden, George, "American Evangelical Scholarship," in *Rationality in the Calvinian Tradition*, ed. Hendrik Hart, Johan van der Hoeven, Nicholas Wolterstorff (Lanham, MD: University Press of America, c1983), 238.

23. Hodge, Charles, *Systematic Theology*, (Massachusetts: Hendrickson Publishers, 1999), 49. Paul Kjoss Helseth writes against the view that the Princeton Theologians were rationalists: "When Old Princeton's 'intellectualism' is interpreted within a context which affirms that the soul is a single unit that acts in all of its functions—its thinking, its feeling, and its willing—as a single substance, it becomes clear that the Princeton theologians were not cold, calculating rationalists" Helseth, Paul Kjoss, "B B Warfield's Apologetical Appeal to 'Right Reason': Evidence of a 'Rather Bald Rationalism'?" in *Scottish Bulletin of Evangelical Theology* 16. (Autumn 1998): 156–177. 157.

24. Hodge, *Systematic*, 49.

25. Hodge, *Systematic*, 49.

26. Hodge, *Systematic*, 49.

27. Hodge, *Systematic*, 49.

28. Hodge, *Systematic*, 191.

29. Hodge, *Systematic*, 191.

30. Hodge, *Systematic*, 191.

31. Hodge, *Systematic*, 191.

32. Hodge, *Systematic*, 192.

33. Hodge, *Systematic*, 192.

34. Hodge, *Systematic*, 52.

35. Hodge, *Systematic*, 52.

36. Hodge, *Systematic*, 52.

37. Hodge, *Systematic*, 52.

38. Hodge, *Systematic*, 51.

39. Here defined as one who accepts only material causes as explanations for events.

40. Hodge, *Systematic*, 50.

41. Hodge, *Systematic*, 50.

42. Theodore P. Letis investigates the relationship between the German view of

textual criticism and the Princeton Theologians in his article "B.B. Warfield, Common-Sense Philosophy and Biblical Criticism." McClanahan in his article "Benjamin B. Warfield: Historian of Doctrine in Defense of Orthodoxy" argues that "Warfield and the Princetonians of his generation approved, introduced in some cases, and employed the principles of biblical criticism, though, one would say, conservatively" McClanahan, James S. "Benjamin B Warfield : Historian of Doctrine in Defense of Orthodoxy 1881–1921." *Affirmation* 6 (Fall 1993): 89–111.

43. Hodge, *Systematic*, 52.
44. Hodge, *Systematic*, 201.
45. Hodge, *Systematic*, 199.
46. Hodge, *Systematic*, 199.
47. Hodge, *Systematic*, 199.
48. Hodge, *Systematic*, 49.
49. Hodge, *Systematic*, 49.
50. Hodge, *Systematic*, 49.
51. Hodge, *Systematic*, 50.
52. Hodge, *Systematic*, 54.
53. Hodge, *Systematic*, 54.
54. Hodge, *Systematic*, 54.
55. Hodge, *Systematic*, 54.

Chapter 3

1. Warfield, *Studies*, 3.
2. Warfield, *Studies*, 4.
3. Warfield, *Studies*, 9.
4. Warfield, *Studies*, 9.
5. See Helseth's article titled: "B.B. Warfield's Apologetics Appeal to 'Right Reason': Evidence of a 'Rather Bald Rationalism'? in which Helseth argues that the Princeton view should not be classified as rationalist.
6. Warfield, *Studies*, 9.
7. Warfield, *Studies*, 9.
8. Warfield, *Studies*, 4.
9. Warfield, *Studies*, 4.
10. Warfield, *Studies*, 109.
11. Warfield, *Studies*, 111.
12. Warfield, *Studies*, 111.
13. Warfield, *Studies*, 111.
14. Warfield, *Studies*, 111.
15. Warfield, *Studies*, 111.
16. Warfield, *Studies*, 111.
17. Warfield, *Studies*, 111.
18. McClanahan, James S, "Benjamin B Warfield : Historian of Doctrine in Defense of Orthodoxy 1881–1921," *Affirmation* 6, (Fall 1993): 89–111. 89.
19. McClanahan, "Benjamin", 89.
20. Warfield, *Studies*, 109.
21. Hodge, A.A. *The Confession of Faith*. (Edinburgh, The Banner of Truth, 1992), 21.

22. Hodge, *The Confession*, 25.
23. Warfield, Benjamin. *The Westminster Assembly and Its Work*. (Grand Rapids: Baker, 2000), 163.
24. Warfield, *The Westminster Assembly*, 163.
25. Warfield, *The Westminster Assembly*, 163.
26. Warfield, *The Westminster Assembly*, 163.
27. Warfield, *The Westminster Assembly*, 379.
28. Warfield, *The Westminster Assembly*, 379.
29. Warfield, *The Westminster Assembly*, 398.
30. Warfield, *The Westminster Assembly*, 398.
31. Warfield, *The Westminster Assembly*, 399.
32. Warfield, *Studies*, 110.
33. For a look at Warfield's relation to textual criticism see the articles by Letis and McClanahan mentioned above.

Chapter 4

1. Warfield, "Introduction," in *Apologetics*, 27.
2. Warfield, "Introduction," in *Apologetics*, 27.
3. Heslam, Peter S, "Architects of Evangelical Intellectual Thought: Abraham Kuyper and Benjamin Warfield," *Themelios* 24, no. 2 (Fall 1999): 3–20.
4. Heslam, "Architects."
5. Van Til, Cornelius, *Defense of the Faith* (Phillipsburg: Presbyterian and Reformed Publishing, 1967), 151.
6. Van Til, *Defense*, 151.
7. Kuyper, Abraham, *Principles of Sacred Theology* (Grand Rapids: Baker Book House, 1980), 348.
8. Kuyper, *Principles*, 151.
9. Kuyper, *Principles*, 381.
10. Kuyper, *Principles*, 381.
11. Kuyper, *Principles*, 381.
12. Donald Fuller and Richard Gardiner locate this as the issue when they say "with the 'death' of classical, *metaphysical* 'first principles of reason' in the nineteenth century due to Hume and Kant, empiricist and transcendental philosophers of science (despite differences) agreed generally in proposing some type of *physical* or naturalistic 'first principle' as the ground for the veracity of their scientific inquiry. That physical 'first principle' was ultimately grounded in this assumption of the uniformity of nature . . . Kant's own transcendental philosophy of science is dependent on this assumption" (Fuller, Donald; Gardiner, Richard, "Reformed Theology at Princeton and Amsterdam in the Late Nineteenth Century: A Reappraisal," *Presbyterion* 21 (Spring 1995): 89–117. 93.
13. Kuyper, *Principles*, 152.
14. Kuyper, *Principles*, 152.
15. Heslam, "Architects."
16. "While Warfield acknowledged that 'rational arguments can of themselves produce nothing more than "historical faith"', he nonetheless insisted that 'historical faith' is 'of no little use in the world' because what the Holy Spirit does in the new birth is not to work 'a ready-made faith, rooted in nothing and clinging without reason to its

object', but rather 'to give to a faith which naturally grows out of the proper grounds of faith, that peculiar quality which makes it saving faith'. Since the Holy Spirit 'does not produce faith without grounds', we can infer that Warfield engaged in apologetics not to argue the unregenerate into the kingdom of God, but rather to facilitate their engagement in the most basic activity of human existence, namely reaction to the truth of God that is reflected into the soul" (Helseth, Paul Kjoss, "B.B. Warfield's Apologetical Appeal to 'Right Reason': Evidence of a 'Rather Bald Rationalism'?", *Scottish Bulletin of Evangelical Theology* 16 (Autumn 1998): 156–177. 177.

17. Kuyper, *Principles*, 154.
18. Kuyper, *Principles*, 154.
19. Kuyper, *Principles*, 154.
20. Kuyper, *Principles*, 155.
21. Kuyper, *Principles*, 155.
22. Kuyper, *Principles*, 155.
23. Kuyper, *Principles*, 155.
24. Kuyper, *Principles*, 157.
25. Kuyper, *Principles*, 157.
26. Kuyper, *Principles*, 157.
27. Kuyper, *Principles*, 158.
28. Kuyper, *Principles*, 159.
29. Kuyper, *Principles*, 166.
30. Kuyper, *Principles*, 172.
31. Kuyper, Abraham. *Lectures on Calvinism* (Grand Rapids: Eerdmans Publishing Company, 1999), 10.
32. Kuyper, *Lectures*, 11.
33. Kuyper, *Lectures*, 18.
34. Kuyper, *Lectures*, 18.
35. Kuyper, *Lectures*, 18.
36. Kuyper, *Lectures*, 19.
37. Kuyper, *Lectures*, 19.
38. Kuyper, *Lectures*, 21.
39. Kuyper, *Principles*, 302.
40. Kuyper, *Principles*, 302.
41. Kuyper, *Principles*, 175.
42. Kuyper, *Principles*, 342.
43. Kuyper, *Principles*, 342.
44. Kuyper, *Principles*, 345.
45. A problem arises for Kuyper when his theory is applied to itself. Kuyper's theory is relative to his worldview, to his science, and hence is not universal, and one must wonder why it should be accepted. Why accept Kuyper's view over the other? Are there any universal/necessary truths? If there are, is not there really only one science, the correct one that uses these truths, and then a whole bunch of bad science? People might try to argue against the laws of thought, but "can" they argue against them? Warfield's view of right reason avoided these sorts of problems.
46. Kuyper, *Principles*, 405.
47. Kuyper, *Principles*, 249.
48. Warfield, *Studies*, 111.
49. Warfield, *Studies*, 111.

50. Warfield, "Introduction" in *Apologetics*, 19.
51. Warfield, "Introduction," in *Apologetics*, 26.
52. Warfield, "Introduction," in *Apologetics*, 26.
53. Warfield, "Introduction," in *Apologetics*, 27.
54. Warfield, "Introduction," in *Apologetics*, 27.
55. Warfield, "Introduction," in *Apologetics,* 27.
56. Warfield, *Studies*, 97.
57. Warfield, *Studies*, 104.
58. Warfield, "Introduction," in *Apologetics*, 25.
59. Warfield, "Introduction," in *Apologetics*, 25.
60. Warfield, "Introduction," in *Apologetics*, 25.
61. Warfield, "Introduction," in *Apologetics*, 25.
62. Warfield, "Introduction," in *Apologetics*, 25.
63. Warfield, "Introduction," in *Apologetics*, 25.
64. Warfield, "Introduction," in *Apologetics*, 27.
65. Warfield, "Introduction," in *Apologetics*, 32.
66. Warfield, "Introduction," in *Apologetics*, 32.
67. Warfield, "Introduction," in *Apologetics*, 20.
68. Warfield, "Introduction," in *Apologetics*, 20.
69. Warfield, "Introduction," in *Apologetics*, 20.
70. Warfield, "Introduction," in *Apologetics*, 20.
71. Warfield, "Introduction," in *Apologetics*, 21.
72. Warfield, "Introduction," in *Apologetics*, 21.
73. Warfield, "Introduction," in *Apologetics*, 24.
74. Warfield, "Introduction," in *Apologetics*, 24.
75. Warfield, "Introduction," in *Apologetics*, 24.
76. Warfield, "Introduction," in *Apologetics*, 24.
77. Warfield, "Introduction," in *Apologetics*, 24.
78. Warfield, "Introduction," in *Apologetics*, 24.
79. Warfield, *Studies*, 97.
80. Donald Fuller and Richard Gardiner summarize this difference when they say "While Old Princeton remained committed to pre-Enlightenment orthodoxy with its *theological* worldview, affirming the *metaphysical first principles of reason*, the Amsterdam school slowly imbibed many aspects of the *anthropocentric*, Kantian worldview and a conception of theology more in line with Fichtian science than classical Christian orthodoxy." (Fuller, "Reformed," 104).

Chapter 5

1. Reid, W. Stanford, "J. Gresham Machen," in *Reformed Theology in America*, ed. David Wells (Grand Rapids: Baker Books, 1997), 97.
2. Reid, "J. Gresham Machen," 97.
3. See also John Frame's *Cornelius Van Til* (1995).
4. Van Til, Cornelius, *Christian Apologetics* (Phillipsburg: Presbyterian and Reformed Publishing, 1976), 1.
5. Van Til, *Christian*, 1.
6. Van Til, *Christian*, 1.
7. Van Til, *Christian*, 2.

8. Bahnsen, Greg L, *Van Til's Apologetic: Readings and Analysis* (Phillipsburg: Presbyterian and Reformed Publishing, 1998), 30.

9. Bahnsen, *Van Til's*, 30.

10. Kant, Immanuel, "Critique of Pure Reason," in *Modern Philosophy*, ed. Forrest E. Baird and Walter Kaufmann (Prentice Hall, New Jersey: 1997), 491–531. 510.

11. Fuller, "Reformed," 92.

12. Fuller, "Reformed," 91.

13. Bahnsen, *Van Til's*, 30.

14. Bahnsen, *Van Til's*, 30.

15. Van Til, *Christian*, 10.

16. Van Til, *Christian*, 96.

17. Bahnsen, *Van Til's*, 30.

18. Bahnsen, *Van Til's*, 61.

19. Bahnsen, *Van Til's*, 61.

20. Bahnsen, *Van Til's*, 6.

21. Bahnsen, *Van Til's*, 6.

22. Bahnsen, *Van Til's*, 6.

23. Bahnsen, *Van Til's*, 6.

24. Bahnsen, *Van Til's*, 6.

25. Bahnsen, *Van Til's*, 95.

26. Van Til, *Christian*, 30.

27. Van Til, *Christian*, 31.

28. Van Til, *Christian*, 31.

29. Bahnsen, *Van Til's*, 187.

30. Bahnsen, *Van Til's*, 192.

31. Helseth argues that Princeton's affirmation of the soul as a single unit implies a connection between knowing, feeling, and willing (Helseth, "B.B. Warfield," 157).

32. Milton, John, *Paradise Lost* (Chicago: Encyclopedia Britannica, 1948), 154.

33. Van Til, *Christian*, 33.

34. Roberts, Wesley A, "Cornelius Van Til," in *Reformed Theology in America* ed. David Wells (Grand Rapids: Baker Books, 1997), 175.

35. Bahnsen, *Van Til's*, 6.

36. Clark is mentioned here because of his strong Reformed heritage and his opposition to Van Til. For more on the debate between Clark and Van Til read: *The Clark-Van Til Controversy* by Herman Hoeksema.

37. Bahnsen, *Van Til's*, 95.

38. Van Til, *Christian*, 2.

39. Bahnsen, *Van Til's*, 597.

40. Bahnsen, *Van Til's*, 598.

41. Bahnsen, *Van Til's*, 598.

42. Bahnsen, *Van Til's*, 598.

43. Bahnsen, *Van Til's*, 598.

44. Bahnsen, *Van Til's*, 598.

45. Bahnsen, *Van Til's*, 599.

46. Bahnsen, *Van Til's*, 599.

47. Bahnsen, *Van Til's*, 601.

48. Bahnsen, *Van Til's*, 600.

49. Bahnsen, *Van Til's*, 608.

50. Bahnsen, *Van Til's*, 608.

51. Warfield, *Studies*, 97.

52. Van Til, Cornelius. *A Survey of Christian Epistemology* (Phillipsburg: Presbyterian and Reformed Publishing), x.

Chapter 6

1. Plantinga, Alvin. *Warranted Christian Belief* (Oxford: Oxford University Press, 2000), 108.

2. Plantinga, *Warranted*, 202.

3. Plantinga, *Warranted*, 202.

4. Plantinga, *Warranted*, 203.

5. Plantinga, *Warranted*, 204.

6. Plantinga, *Warranted*, 205.

7. Plantinga, *Warranted*, 3.

8. Plantinga, *Warranted*, 93.

9. Plantinga, *Warranted*, 99.

10. Plantinga, *Warranted*, 101.

11. Plantinga, *Warranted*, 359.

12. Plantinga, *Warranted*, 363.

13. Plantinga, *Warranted*, 367.

14. Plantinga, *Warranted*, 367.

15. Plantinga, *Warranted*, 317.

16. Plantinga, *Warranted*, 317.

17. Clark, Kelly James. *Return to Reason*. William B. Eerdmans Publishing Company, Grand Rapids: 1990

18. Tilley, Terrence. "Reformed Epistemology and Religious Fundamentalism: How Basic Are Our Basic Beliefs?" *Modern Theology*, 6:3 April 1990. 237–257.

19. Plantinga, *Warranted*, 198.

Chapter 7

1. For an in-depth analysis and exploration of each of these steps, see Surrendra Gangadean's *Philosophical Foundation: A Critical Analysis of Basic Beliefs*, (Lanham, University Press of America, 2008).

2. Edwards, Jonathan. The Works of Jonathan Edwards. Volume 1. (Peabody, Hendrickson: 1998), 690.

3. Locke, John. *An Essay Concerning Human Understanding*. Ed. P.H. Nidditch. (Oxford, Clarendon Press: 1979), IV.10.1.20.

4. Locke, *Essay*, IV.10.1.11.

5. Locke, *Essay*, IV.18.10.1.

6. Locke, *Essay*, IV.18.7.5.

7. Locke, *Essay*, IV.18.11.16.

8. Locke, *The Reasonableness of Christianity*, ed. John C. Higgins-Biddle, (Oxford, Clarendon Press: 2000), 11.

9. Higgins-Biddle, John C. Introduction, *The Reasonableness of Christianity*, xxi.

10. Locke, *Reasonableness*, 6.

Chapter 8

1. Warfield, Studies in Theology, 110.
2. Warfield, Studies in Theology, 110.
3. Warfield, Studies in Theology, 110.
4. Reymond, Robert L. *The Justification of Knowledge: An Introductory Study of Christian Apologetic Methodology* (Pittsburg: Presbyterian and Reformed Publishing Company, 1976), 61.
5. Warfield, Benjamin B. "The Real Problem of Inspiration" in *Revelation and Inspiration*. Baker Book House, Grand Rapids, 2000. (218).
6. Reymond, *Justification*, 67.
7. Warfield, *Studies*, 110.
8. Sennett, James F. and Douglas Groothius. *In Defense of Natural Theology: A Post-Humean Assessment*, (Downers Grove: Intervarsity Press, 2005). 15.
9. Hume, David. *Hume's Enquiries*, Sect X, Part II, 100.
10. Hume, David. *A Treatise of Human Nature*, (Dover: Mineola, 2003) 53.
11. Hume, Hume's Enquiries, Sect IV, Part I, 20.
12. Kant, Immanuel. "Critique of Theistic Proofs" in *Classical and Contemporary Readings in the Philosophy of Religion*, ed. John Hick (Prentice Hall: Upper Saddle River, 1990), 140.
13. Kant, *Critique*, 126.
14. John 17:3.

GLOSSARY OF TERMS

a priori   What is known apart from experience, perhaps due to be self-evident or derived from self-evident principles.

Alexander,   A founding professor of Princeton Theological Seminary in 1812.
Archibald   He was influenced by the Rev. William Graham, a president of
(1772–1851)   Princeton College. Before teaching at Princeton he served as the president of Hampden-Sydney College.

anathema   To be banned and excommunicated due to conflict with what is orthodox.

apologetics   Based on the Greek word *apologia*, it is a defense of one's beliefs. In 1 Peter 3:15 the word is used to encourage Christians to be ready to give a defense for the hope they have. Classically, when Socrates was put on trial by the Athenians his defense was recorded by Plato in what is now called The Apology. To give a defense is to give reasons for one's conclusion.

apostasy   The abandonment of one's religion.

Aquinas,   A Roman Catholic philosopher, he is best known as the great sys-
Thomas   tematizer of medieval scholastic philosophy. He incorporated
(1224/25–1274) Aristotle's philosophy, believing that it represented the best of what can be known about nature, and that Christianity adds grace and special revelation. His "5 Ways" for proving the existence of God continue to be relied upon.

argument   The third act of reason (see concept and judgment) in which premises are used to logically support a conclusion (see validity and soundness).

Augustine   The last of the early Church Fathers, with Augustine the era of the
(354–430)   early Church comes to an end. He incorporated Plato's philosophy into understanding God and the goal of the Christian life.

basic belief	A belief is basic in relation to another if it is assumed by that belief. For example, Christianity assumes that God exists, God's existence assumes that something is eternal. The most basic beliefs are those that are assumed by other beliefs but do not themselves have assumptions.
beatific vision	The direct vision of God enjoyed by the blessed in heaven.
Calvin, John (1509–1564)	A Reformer who focused attention on the sovereignty of God in all areas of life. The "Five Points of Calvinism" are based on his theology.
Calvinism	The theological system of Calvin and his followers. It focused attention on the sovereignty of God in all areas of life, including in soteriology.
casuist	Case based reasoning and application of rules to particular instances.
Christian worldview	The worldview based on the topics of creation, fall, and redemption. Under "creation" is includes the clarity of general revelation, in order to make sense of the Fall and the need for redemption.
clarity	Applied to basic beliefs; a belief is clear to reason if the contradiction is not logically or existentially possible; e.g., there must be something eternal; clarity is necessary for meaning, morality and inexcusability; one knows what is clear if one can show what is clear; what is clear can be known by anyone who seeks to know.
common sense (source of skepticism)	Takes appearance for reality: the sun rises in the east; the earth is flat; the color of the ocean is blue; there is an external world; based on what is common to sense perception, rather than common sense as practical wisdom; it takes the condition/position of the perceiver for granted.
common sense (cultural)	What is commonly agreed upon in a culture and therefore appears to be beyond questioning to persons in that culture.
concept	The first act of reason (see judgment and argument); in a concept the mind grasps the essence of a thing or class of things; set in contrast to an image, an act of the senses; concepts are either well-formed or not.
contradiction	Contradictory statements differ in quantity (all or some) and quality (is or is not); they cannot both be true and they cannot both be false at the same time; *all s is p* is contradicted by *some s is not p*; *no s is p* is contradicted by *some s is p* (see judgment).
creation *ex nihilo*	Affirmed by historic theism, it is the belief that God created the world out of no pre-existing substance; in contrast to dualism

where creation is by forming pre-existing matter, and to panthe-ism—in which the world is a part of God; it is the basis of affirm-ing the infinite power and wisdom of God.

de jure objection   The objection to Christian belief which claims that Christian belief is irrational, or in some other way intellectually problematic.

defeaters   A question that undermines the justification for a belief or conclu-sion.

deism   Belief that the world was created by God but not actively ruled by God; God did not act after creation to bring about natural evil in the world or to give any redemptive revelation to mankind (Vol-taire and Thomas Jefferson).

didactic   Something intended to teach, or convey information.

dogmatic   Beliefs that are accepted as orthodox and authoritative. This can become a negative designation when such beliefs are asserted as true but not in need of supporting proof.

dominion   The exercise of rule or authority given to mankind to develop the powers latent in oneself and in the creation; based on the principle that creation is revelation, it is directed toward the good as knowl-edge of God; set in contrast to domination as rule for self-interest.

doxological   Pertaining to the praise of the glory of God.

dualism   The ontological position that reality consists of two distinct kinds of being—matter and spirit—both of which are eternal; affirmed in different forms of Greek thought by Plato and Aristotle; distinct from theism, although dualistic attitudes persist in popular forms of theism.

Dutch Neo-Calvinist   Relying on the work of Abraham Kuyper, this movement seeks to have every area of life influenced by Christianity, including the affects of Modernity.

Edwards, Jonathan (1703–1758)   Thought to be the greatest American philosopher and theologian, and responsible for the First Great Awakening. His Sermon "Sin-ners in the Hands of an Angry God" addressed persons who had not yet experienced an inner conviction of a need for change.

Emerson, Ralph Waldo (1803–1882)   American intellectual and founder of Transcendentalism. This view teaches that there is a spiritual state that transcends the mate-rial world and is only realizable through intuition.

empiricism   The epistemological position that all knowledge arises from sense experience; affirmed by John Locke; Hume drew out its skeptical implications; assumed uncritically in some claims made in the name of science; radical empiricism includes inner as well as sense experience.

Enlightenment   The Enlightenment began roughly around 1648, after the end of the Wars of Religion, and sought to find a natural religion that all humans could agree to and would avoid the strife engendered by revealed religion. Its motto, expressed by Immanuel Kant, was "dare to reason."

epistemology   Theory of knowledge; a major branch of philosophy that deals with the questions "Is knowledge possible?" and "How do I know?"

essence   The set of qualities that all members and only members of a class always have; human essence is said to be both rational and animal.

eternal life   Christians believe that eternal life is knowing God (John 17:3).

**eternal power   What St. Paul says can be known of God from general revelation
& divine nature**   (Romans 1:18-20). This is a full knowledge about God's existence and nature, as opposed to a bare knowledge of God as a "prime mover."

ethics   Ethics is concerned with giving a rational justification for an answer to the question "What is the good?" Ethics assumes choice which assumes values and therefore the highest value which is the good; what is sought in ethics is rational justification for one's view of the good.

**evidentialist /   The system of apologetics which attempts to establish Christian
evidentialism**   belief through empirical evidences. These can be external evidences, such as miracles, historical evidence, cultural evidence, and changed lives. Or these can be inner evidences, such as feelings, intuitions, and personal testimonies.

**evolution,   A purely natural explanation of the development from non-life to
naturalistic**   life, to more complex life, to hominid, to human; macro—not micro—evolution; internal disputes exist over gradual vs. non-gradual process; external challenges exist over the scientific vs. philosophical status of evolution.

**evolution,   A synthesis of naturalistic evolution and belief in God; subject to
theistic**   criticism from both naturalists and theists as compromising essential features of each and is therefore inadequate as a compromise position; it has been subject to revision in the direction of theism or naturalism.

faith   Faith is applied to belief in general which cannot be verified through sense experience; faith is not opposed to reason; as truth cannot be separated from meaning, faith cannot be separated from reason; faith grows as understanding grows; it is tested as understanding is tested.

faith seeking understanding
A saying attributed to St. Anselm. It implies that one believes something, but does not understand what one believes. It is in contrast to the claim that faith is understanding, that one can only believe to the extent that one understands.

Fall
Referring to the event in Genesis 3 when Adam and Eve fell from the state of innocence. This was a result of believing the tempter, which was a result of failing to seek to know God. The eating of the fruit required that Adam and Eve believe that they could be like God, which is something they could have known to be false from general revelation.

fideism
Holding a belief without proof; proof is seen either as not relevant or not possible or may not actually be present; belief may be either theistic or non-theistic; fideism assumes basic things are not clear; belief without proof based on understanding loses of all meaning.

foundation
Those beliefs that are essential to a worldview and assumed by the other parts of the worldview.

foundationalism
The epistemology which seeks to ground all knowledge on foundational truths which are not in need of further proof. The problem is in identifying which truths these are, and explaining why they are not in need of further proof.

freedom
Doing what I want or please or choose, all things considered; applied to the most basic level of thought, I can use my reason if I want to; set in contrast to libertarian freedom: if ought implies can, then can assumes want; the want of a rational agent is always free.

general revelation
What can be known of God at all times and by all persons through the ordinary means of knowing; in contrast to special revelation; the subject matter of natural vs. revealed religion. It is "general" in the sense of being "universal."

German pantheism
A belief that became influential through the works of the philosopher Hegel in the 19th century. It is a form of the claim that "all is God."

good and necessary consequence
An inference of reason; what must be said, if other things are accepted as true; applied to analyzing concepts, judgments and arguments; used in critical, interpretive and constructive reasoning.

happiness
The effect of possessing what one believes to be the good; not sought for its own sake as the good but naturally accompanying the possessing what is believed to be of highest value; lasting

happiness is the effect of possessing what truly is the good.

Harvard Founded in 1636 by puritans in Massachusetts. It held as one of its entrance qualifications that the students seek to glorify God. It has gone through a number of religious and philosophical changes, so that by the 19th century it was Unitary rather than Reformed Protestant.

hedonism The ethical view that pleasure/happiness of one kind or another is the good (Epicurus, Mill).

Heraclitus (540–480) Greek philosopher who believed that "all is change" or "all is in a state of flux."

hermeneutics The process by which the meaning of a text or an event is understood; no experience is meaningful without interpretation; in general we interpret what is less basic in light of what is more basic; we interpret our experience in light of our basic belief or worldview assumptions.

heuristic The process of learning or discovering; often associated with solving a problem.

Historic Christianity What has come to be agreed upon by the pastor/teachers after much discussion. The first model of this is in Acts 15, then the Apostles' Creed, and then the Nicene Creed. The most recent example is the Westminster Confession of Faith.

Hodge, A.A. (1823–1886) Son of Charles Hodge, and named after A. Alexander, taught at Princeton for ten years.

Hodge, Charles (1797–1878) Taught at Princeton from 1822 until 1878, with an exception of two years spent studying in Germany. His *Systematic Theology* replaced Turretin's *Institutio Theologiae Elencticae* at Princeton as the text for theology.

Hume, David (1711–1776) Scottish philosopher. His empiricism led him to challenge earlier philosophers, such as John Locke, that he did not believe had been consistent in their empiricism. He also challenges religious belief as being contrary to reason.

Idealism The belief that only minds and ideas exist.

induction Reasoning from observation of instances of things to a general statement about that class of things; from observing that some crows are black to the general statement that all crows are black.

inexcusable / unexcusable / inexcusability To be without excuse. A person is inexcusable in believing something if that belief is clearly false. One is inexcusable for not believing something if it is clearly true, or its contradiction is clearly false. See "clarity".

intuition

An immediate awareness one has, apart from reason and the senses, of the connection between a (natural) sign and what it signifies; e.g., smile and friendliness, beauty and goodness; misleading if one thinks the sign is the reality, or that the sign is always accompanied by the reality.

judgment

The second act of reason in which two concepts are joined by affirmation or separated by negation: *all s is p, no s is p, some s is p, some s is not p;* judgments are either true or false and may be simple or complex; a statement is used to express a judgment (or proposition).

justified / justification

In epistemology: a reason given in support of a conclusion. In soteriology: a person is justified before God when that person's sins are imputed to Christ, and Christ's righteousness is imputed to that person.

Kant, Immanuel (1724–1804)

German philosopher who began his career accepting a kind of Christian rationalism articulated by Christina Wolff, but then rejected this after reading the criticisms of David Hume. His solution to Hume's challenges was to distinguish the world as experience from the world in itself, and to argue that the human mind shapes the way that the world in itself is experienced. One implication is that the human can never know what the world in itself is like because all experiences are shaped by the human mind.

knowledge

Knowledge is distinguished from opinion and falsehood. This is attained when a person has a true, justified belief.

knowledge of God

This is said by Christ to be eternal life (John 17:3). Some persons assert that this knowledge is direct and intuitive. But when such knowledge is questioned, it requires a response, which requires the work of inferences. Furthermore, God is not known directly, but by His works. Thus all knowledge of God is inferential rather than direct.

Kuyper, Abraham (1837–1920)

Born in 1837 in Maassluis, a seaport town in the Netherlands. In 1855 Kuyper entered the University of Leiden. After this Kuyper spent some time in the ministry, until 1874 when he was elected to the Second Chamber and began his career in politics. Between 1880 and 1901 he taught theology at a university he had helped to found—the Free University of Amsterdam. In 1901-1905 he rose to be prime minister in the second Antirevolutionary Cabinet. In 1898 he was the guest speaker at the Stone Lectures at Princeton where he gave what have come to be known as his *Lectures on Calvinism.*

laws of thought

Identity: *a* is *a*. Non-contradiction: not both *a* and *non-a*. Excluded Middle: either *a* or *non-a*.

liberal /   Originally the view that sought to allow people to think for them-
liberalism   selves rather than being restricted by tradition, it came to be set in
                      opposition to orthodoxy.

libertarianism   A view of freedom where *ought* implies *can*; one is free if one
                      could have done otherwise; related to causality, if my act was
                      caused, it could not have been otherwise; libertarianism denies
                      determinism (every event is caused) in order to affirm freedom
                      (Kant, William James).

light of man /   A metaphor likening light which illuminates objects for the eyes to
light of nature   reason which illuminates reality for the mind.

literalism   The belief that understanding a text is free of interpretive assump-
                      tions; that preceding layers of context are not necessarily relevant;
                      that meaning is explicit only and not also by inference; that under-
                      standing language figuratively is to be avoided whenever possible.

Locke, John   British philosopher who advocated empiricism. He also sought
(1632–1704)   natural principles that could serve as the basis for civil govern-
                      ment.

logos   Greek term translated in John 1:1 as "Word." The *logos* is the
                      explanation, or reason for, or what makes something known. It is
                      used as a suffix in words like "biology," "anthropology," and "the-
                      ology."

Machen,   One of the founding professors of Westminster Theological Semi-
J. Gresham   nary. He left Princeton Seminary when he believed it had unal-
(1881–1937)   terably abandoned its original mission and beliefs.

Manichaeism   A form of Greek dualism which tried to incorporate some Chris-
                      tian language, and taught that spirit is good while matter is evil.

material   The belief that all is matter and matter is eternal.
monism

meaning /   A claim is meaningful if it obeys the laws of thought, and where
meaningless-   these laws are violated there is no meaning. Persons could be in a
ness   state of meaninglessness in the sense that the world is meaningless
                      to them.

metaphysics   A branch of philosophy which deals with the question, "What is
                      real or eternal?"; it deals with *ontology*—the nature of being,
                      whether being is matter or spirit; it deals with *cosmology*—how
                      the cosmos came to be.

modern   Spoken of by theologians like Kuyper to refer to the combination
worldview   of materialism and empiricism which sought to replace the Chris-
                      tian worldview.

modernism The belief in the material success of humanity through institutions such as capitalism and democracy, and based on the work of science and the epistemology of empiricism.

modernity A time period after the Wars of Religion until the World Wars of the 20th century.

Molinism The belief that the problem of evil can be solved by claiming that God looks into the future and selects which world to create based on future outcomes. Thus, while there is evil in this world, there is no other world that contains more good and less evil. It assumes a libertarian view of freedom, and that God must look into the future to see what agents will do, rather than determining what will come about to the praise of His glory through the act of creation.

moral evil An act contrary to the nature of one's being; for man as a rational being it is to neglect, avoid, resist or deny reason in the face of what is clear; it is the failure to seek and to understand and to do what is right.

moral law What is required of man in order to achieve the good.

mysticism The belief that a special inner experience is required to know the highest reality.

natural principle Kuyper used this to refer to thinking about humans apart from God.

natural theology The product of the study of general revelation.

natural evil In the context of an all-powerful and all-good Creator, natural evil is not original in the creation, nor inherent in moral evil; it is imposed by God to restrain, recall from and to remove moral evil; it consists in toil and strife, and old age, sickness and death and all amplifications of these in famine, war and plague.

naturalism The worldview of material monism: only natural forces explain all phenomena of nature; applied to human culture, it is called secular humanism: only human effort explains all social phenomena; in the sciences, methodological naturalism in explanation (all knowledge is through sense experience) is used to support metaphysical naturalism—there is no God, no spirit or soul and no afterlife.

necessary truths What must be true because the contradiction is not possible.

neo-orthodox Based on the work of Karl Barth, this claims that while scripture is not inerrant, God works through the reading of scripture to bring people to Him.

neutral / common ground	What can be agreed upon by everyone, or what is used by everyone. Common ground need not be neutral in the sense of supporting all beliefs; indeed, it might be that what is common to all provides the basis for only one specific set of beliefs.
nihilism	The loss of all meaningful distinctions in epistemology, metaphysics and ethics; the inherent consequence of skepticism—the denial of all clarity; a position which cannot be maintained with integrity.
non- cognitivism	The claim that the meaning of propositions is not cognitive.
non- contradiction (law of)	Not both *a* and *non-a*.
ontology	The study of the nature of being.
paganism	The belief in polytheism or shamanism, and the accompanying superstitions.
palingenesis (rebirth)	The act of the Holy Spirit to bring a person from spiritual death to spiritual life.
philosophy	Philosophy can be defined in terms of its several features: *area*—foundation and goal; *attitude*—love of wisdom; *method*—critical use of reason; *application*—self-examination; *system*—a worldview.
Platonism	Plato's philosophy took as basic the distinction between the material world which is in a state of change, and the ideal world which is unchanging. To attain knowledge one must have a direct vision of the ideal world, apart from the body and matter. While in the body, one will always be prone to error.
polemics	The study of disputation and refutation of opponents.
pragmatism	A theory of truth: a belief is true if it yields satisfactory consequences (if it works); also a theory of meaning: the meaning of a belief is the conduct it is fitted to produce (W. James); claims to settle metaphysical disputes; assumes skepticism and that what works is common ground.
presupposition	What is assumed or presupposed in any given statement or belief; applied particularly to what is assumed in a person's *system* of beliefs or worldview; one's most basic belief about what is eternal.
presupposi- tionalism	The system of apologetics which seeks to identify and analyze the presuppositions of worldviews.

Princeton College	Founded in 1746 by the New Side, a debate about the extent to which ministers must adhere to creedal standards
Princeton Seminary	Founded in 1812 in the "old light/old light" debate. This debate was about the confessional requirements for ministers, and the role of personal conversion experience in the Christian life.
problem of evil	If God is all good and all powerful, why is there evil?; if God is all powerful he could create a world without evil; if he is all good he would create a world without evil; the problem is intellectual, to make sense of an apparent contradiction, and not empty basic terms of meaning.
proof / argument / inference	In an inference a conclusion is drawn from supporting premises. These premises are said to be the proof, or argument, for the conclusion. In a valid argument, if the premises are true the conclusion will be true (and each follows the rules of inference). In a sound argument the argument is valid and the premises are true.
proper / improper function	An externalist theory of knowledge. Persons are said to be properly functioning if their epistemic equipment leads to the conclusions intended by the design plan in the appropriate kind of environment. This can be evaluated without needing to ask persons for an internal perspective of why they came to a specific conclusion.
Ramanuja (1017–1137)	Hindu philosopher who criticized Advaita Vedanta and instead gave the system of qualified non-dualism in which all is one, and that one is made up of parts.
rational presupposi- tionalism	Thinking is presuppositional; we think of the less basic in light of the more basic: less basic/more basic, truth/meaning, experience/basic belief, conclusion/premises, finite/infinite, etc.; reason is the test for meaning; if we agree on what is more basic we can agree on what is less basic.
rationalism	A reliance on reason as the source of knowing the truth; to be contrasted with reliance on sense experience or intuition or testimony; also to be contrasted with reliance on reason as a test for meaning.
realism	The view which maintains that the material world exists apart from minds or perception.
reason / right reason / rationality / reasonable	Reason can be denied in itself, its use, and in us (see below). A person is using right reason if the laws of reason are not violated. This can also be what is meant by saying a person or claim is rational/reasonable, although sometimes these simply mean "in accord with common sense."

reason in its use
Reason in its use is *formative*—used to form concepts, judgments and arguments which are the forms of all thought; *critical*—used as a test of meaning; *interpretive*—used to interpret experience in light of basic belief; and *constructive*—used to construct a coherent worldview.

reason in itself
Reason in itself is the laws of thought: the law of identity—*a is a*; the law of non-contradiction—*not both a and non-a*; the law of excluded middle—*either a or non-a*; these laws make thinking possible; the common ground for all who think.

reason in us
Reason in us is *natural*—the same in all thinkers; *ontological*—applies to being as well as to thought; *transcendental*—authoritative, self-attesting, cannot be questioned but makes questioning possible; and *fundamental*—to all other aspects of human personality.

redemptive revelation
Scripture as redemptive revelation reveals how man is brought out of sin and death; scripture assumes all have sinned—no one seeks, no one understands, no one is righteous; all are in the state of spiritual death— meaninglessness, boredom and guilt; redemption by vicarious atonement shows both divine justice and mercy.

Reformation
Beginning in 1517 when Martin Luther objected to the practice of indulgences and the teaching about purgatory. A call for consistency with the teachings of Scripture culminated in the Westminster confession of Faith in 1648. The Puritans were a product of the Reformation, and therefore it has had significant impact on the formation and continuation of the U.S.

Reformed epistemology
The view which claims that Christian belief is warranted because it is the product of proper functioning. It is an attempt to respond to critics who claim that Christian belief is intellectually deficient or irrational.

regeneration
The work of the Holy Spirit in bringing a person from spiritual death to spiritual life.

Reid, Thomas (1710–1796)
Scottish philosopher. He attended Marischal College in Aberdeen, and later taught at King's College in Aberdeen. He is known for his defense of common sense against David Hume's skepticism.

Schleiermacher, Friedrich (1768–1834)
German theologian who sought to reply to Hume by emphasizing the role of experience in knowing God.

science
The attempt to increase knowledge of reality based on theory confirmed by observation in experiment; science is overextended and becomes a source of skepticism when it assumes empiricism, that

all knowledge is from sense experience, or makes claims which go beyond experience.

Scottish Common Sense Philosophy The Scottish Enlightenment taught that knowledge can be achieved by basing beliefs on commonly held assumptions found in all cultures and held by all individuals. The problem is in actually identifying these.

self-deception The act of deceiving oneself about the extent to which one has actually been seeking, understanding, and doing what is right.

self-evident What proves itself. The self-evident is not in need of further proof because it makes proof possible. Example: the law of non-contradiction.

sensus divinitatis The immediate awareness of divinity present in human consciousness; variously understood ranging from a sense of dependence on a higher power to awareness of God as creator and ruler or as one having an innate sense of the qualities of infinite, eternal and unchanging which can only, upon analysis, be applied to God.

Shankara Hindu philosopher who articulated the view known as Advaita Vedanta. This states that all is one without parts.

sin Not seeking, not understanding, and not doing what is right.

skepticism The epistemological view that knowledge is not possible, that nothing is clear; consistently held skepticism leads to nihilism, the loss of all meaning. There is metaphysical, epistemological, hermeneutical, and methodological skepticism.

Sola Scriptura A principle of authority which maintains that scripture is the only rule of faith and life; set in contrast to new revelations of the Spirit or traditions of men; not set in contrast to reason making inferences from scripture, nor to reason making judgments concerning circumstances common to human societies.

soteriology / soteriological The study of, or pertaining to, salvation.

special revelation What is known of God through testimony and its transmission; usually contained in form of scripture; the subject matter of revealed theology in contrast to natural theology or religion.

spiritual monism The ontological position that all of reality is eternal and is spirit; set in contrast to material monism, dualism and theism; matter only *appears* to exist; this reality may be absolute non-dual, beyond all qualities (Shankara) or qualified non-dual, where all is part of God (Ramanuja).

spiritual death   Set in contrast to and analogous to physical death; the inward con-
                         dition of meaninglessness, boredom and guilt; inherent in moral
                         evil as the failure to seek and to understand basic things that are
                         clear to reason.

starting   See "foundation".
principle(s)

systematic   The attempt to build a logically coherent structure (system) of
theology   theology that addresses all relevant topics. What counts as relevant
                         will be relative to one's foundation.

theism   Belief in God the Creator who brought the universe and all things
                         in it into being; God is a Spirit, infinite, eternal, and unchangeable,
                         in his being, wisdom, power, holiness, justice, goodness and truth;
                         in contrast to deism, God in theism is both Creator and ruler of
                         over mankind in history.

theology   The study of God, which makes as its subject what can be known
                         of God through the works of God.

tradition   A way of life handed down by and received on the basis of testi-
                         mony in contrast to reason, intuition or sense experience; without
                         critical analysis, traditions are affirmed to be equal, requiring radi-
                         cal pluralism, diversity, multiculturalism, cultural relativism and
                         tolerance.

transcendental   The argument for God's existence which claims that all knowl-
argument   edge claims presuppose the existence of God.

transcendental-   Arising in the 19th century, stressing the unity of all being, good-
ism   ness of man, and intuition vs. logic.

unbelief   The rejection of the existence of God, or replacement with an
                         alternative concept of God.

Unitarianism   The belief that the deity exists in only one person, arose among
                         Congregationalists ministers influenced by Arian Christology and
                         Arminian Theology.

Van Til,   Born in Grootegast, Holland. At age ten he left from Rotterdam
Cornelius   for the U.S. and settled with his family at Highland, Indiana. In
(1895–1987)   1914 he began attending Calvin Preparatory School and College.
                         In 1921 he enrolled at Calvin Theological Seminary. He trans-
                         ferred in 1922 to Princeton, where he studied both at the seminary
                         and the university. In 1927 he earned a Ph.D in philosophy, and
                         lectured at the seminary from 1928-29. In 1929 Van Til became
                         one of the founding professors at Westminster Theological Semi-
                         nary where he taught for more than 40 years. He is known for his
                         "presuppositional" approach to apologetics.

Warfield, Benjamin (1851–1921)

Born at Grasmere, Kentucky in 1851. He entered the College of New Jersey at Princeton in 1868, and graduated with highest honors in 1871. Before entering the Theological Seminary of the Presbyterian Church at Princeton in 1873 he spent some time traveling in Europe. He was licensed to preach in 1875, but shortly after this was married and then spent some time studying at Leipsic. In 1876 he began teaching at Western Theological Seminary. However, upon the death of A.A. Hodge he was called to teach at Princeton Theological, where he was a professor from 1877 until his death in 1921.

warrant / warranted

A belief that is the product of proper function and is not under question due to a defeater.

Westminster Confession of Faith

Finished in 1648, it was authoritative and influential on Reformed Churches in England and the Colonies.

Westminster Shorter Catechism

A series of questions and answers based on the information in the Westminster Confession of Faith. Intended to help people grow in their maturity and understanding.

Word of God

Spoken of in five senses in John 1: The eternal Son of God; as the light of man—reason; as revealed in creation; as given by the prophets; incarnate as Jesus Christ.

worldview

How a person understands the world based on answers to the basic questions; each culture is shaped by a worldview held more or less consciously and consistently; a culture grows or declines as its worldview increases or decreases in its capacity to provide meaning.

Yale

It was founded in 1701 and is the third oldest university in the United States. Founded based on strict puritan standards.

INDEX

a priori, 53, 99
Abraham, 18, 85
Alexander, A., 3, 12
alternative to heaven, 104
Apostles' Creed, 68
Aquinas, Thomas, 68, 84
Aristotle, 14
atonement, 68, 93, 95
Augustine, 4, 29-33, 72, 73, 78, 84, 99

Bacon, Francis, 12
Bahnsen, Greg, 52-54, 62, 65, 85
Barth, Karl, 84
beatific vision, 30, 36, 85, 104
Belgic Confession, 104
Berkeley, 12, 83, 91
blessed life, 27, 29, 30-32, 79, 99, 104
born again, 44
Buddhism, 40, 82

Calvin, John, 4, 6, 29, 68, 78
Calvinism, 40, 41
Certainty, 13, 14, 42, 87, 94, 98
challenge(s), 4, 98, 100, 102-106
Christian worldview, 4, 6, 7, 40, 45-47, 52, 55, 56, 59, 61, 67, 88, 96, 100, 105
clarity, 2, 3, 6, 9, 11, 15, 19, 21, 23-28, 31, 32, 35, 36, 41-44, 51, 56-59, 61, 64, 87, 88, 96, 97, 103-105
Clark, Gordon, 60, 74
Clark, Kelly James, 74

common sense, 3, 4, 6, 12, 14, 22, 37, 42, 45, 47, 49, 50, 83, 94, 96, 99, 103
conversion, 6, 8, 31, 32, 45, 71, 76, 80, 82

Darwin/ism, 40, 54, 63
de jure, 68-70
defeaters, 67, 68, 70-73
deism, 92
Descartes, Rene, 83, 102
dualism, 24, 61, 83, 86, 91
Dutch neo-Calvinist, 54

Edwards, Jonathan, 69, 71, 72, 74, 76, 93-95
Emerson, Ralph Waldo, 3, 29
empiricism, 12, 14, 82, 83, 86, 89
Enlightenment, 12, 54, 68, 74, 83, 91
epistemology, 1-5, 11, 22, 36, 52, 59, 63, 64, 103
eternal life, 68, 95, 96, 104, 105
eternal power & divine nature, 4, 18-20, 24, 26, 28, 31, 57, 59, 60, 63, 98, 99
evident to the senses, 13, 69
evidentialist/ism, 3, 61, 98, 99
examined life, 1, 71, 75, 77

faith seeking understanding, 86

Reid, Thomas, 4, 12-14, 22, 37,39, 42,
47, 50, 51, 54, 64, 99
religious experience, 43, 70, 71
right reason, 1, 3, 5, 25, 39, 42, 47, 60,
63, 97
Roman Catholicism, 41
Romans, 1, 2, 24, 27, 78, 87, 98, 99

Samadhi, 83
Schleiermacher, Friedrich, 28, 29
science, 5, 12, 22, 26, 35, 38, 39, 42-
49, 54-56, 61-63, 83, 84
Scottish Common Sense Philosophy, 9,
12, 45, 47
self-deception, 58, 59
self-evident, 13, 54, 69, 79, 83
sensus divinitatis, 58, 68, 71-74, 76, 77,
81, 98, 103
Shankara, 83, 91
sin, 2, 6, 19, 22, 25, 28, 30-32, 37, 41-
45, 57, 61, 65, 68, 77, 79, 82, 87, 93
skepticism, 4
Sola Scriptura, 81
soteriology/gical, 68
special revelation, 2, 4, 16-18, 20, 21,
23-28, 31, 32, 37, 39, 43, 44, 46, 48,
49, 51, 57, 68, 80, 85, 90, 92-94
Spinoza, Benedict, 83
spiritual death, 90, 92
spiritual monism, 24, 40, 41
Sproul, R.C., 52
starting principle(s), 5, 52, 101
states of consciousness, 13
Stone lectures, 13, 40
systematic theology, 12, 15, 21, 24

temptation, 30, 43, 72-75, 79, 95
theistic proofs, 24, 76, 96-98, 100, 102,
105
thinking, 7, 18, 23, 101, 103
and Kuyper, 36, 40
and Reid, 14
and Hodge, 21
and Warfield, 22, 28
transcendental argument, 55, 56, 64
Trinity, 93
ontological, 55

unbelief, 1-6, 9, 13, 19-21, 26, 29, 31,
51, 58, 61-63, 68, 75, 78, 81, 87, 88,
95, 98-100, 103, 105
Unitarianism, 3, 10

VanTil, Cornelius, 5, 22, 51-61, 97,
100
the word of God, 85
and *sensus divinitatis*, 81
and Princeton, 64
and circular reasoning, 63
worldview, 62, 63
reason, 36

Warfield, Benjamin, 1, 42
and apologetics, 37, 52, 53
epistemology, 57, 59
experience of God, 100
first principles, 49
Holy Spirit, 56
intuitive knowledge, 97, 105
objectivity, 62
Princeton, 81
probability, 62
right reason, 45, 47, 50, 60, 61, 63
sin, 44, 72, 73
worldview, 46
warrant, 67, 75, 79, 84, 96
warranted, 6, 67-72, 81, 84, 101
Westminster Confession of Faith, 9-10,
21, 25, 52, 78, 82, 104
Westminster Shorter Catechism, 25, 29,
31, 71
Witherspoon, John, 11
Wolterstorff, Nicholas, 96
Word of God, eternal, 60
John 1, 60
worldview(s), 1, 5, 7, 13
naturalist, 17
apologetics, 22
non-theistic, 24
and Kuyper, 36
two basic worldviews, 37
and rationality, 46, 53
and presuppositions, 54, 64
theistic worldview, 55
and knowledge, 57
inexcusable, 59
materialist, 61